ROUTLEDGE LIBRARY EDITIONS: ENERGY ECONOMICS

Volume 18

THE EFFECT OF ENERGY SUPPLY ON ECONOMIC GROWTH

THE EFFECT OF ENERGY SUPPLY ON ECONOMIC GROWTH

E. VICTOR NIEMEYER

Routledge
Taylor & Francis Group

LONDON AND NEW YORK

First published in 1984 by Garland Publishing, Inc.

This edition first published in 2018
by Routledge
2 Park Square, Milton Park, Abingdon, Oxon OX14 4RN

and by Routledge
711 Third Avenue, New York, NY 10017

Routledge is an imprint of the Taylor & Francis Group, an informa business

British Library Cataloguing in Publication Data
A catalogue record for this book is available from the British Library

ISBN: 978-1-138-10476-1 (Set)
ISBN: 978-1-315-14526-6 (Set) (ebk)
ISBN: 978-1-138-50129-4 (Volume 18) (hbk)
ISBN: 978-1-315-14426-9 (Volume 18) (ebk)

Publisher's Note
The publisher has gone to great lengths to ensure the quality of this reprint but points out that some imperfections in the original copies may be apparent.

Disclaimer
The publisher has made every effort to trace copyright holders and would welcome correspondence from those they have been unable to trace.

The Effect
of Energy Supply
on Economic Growth

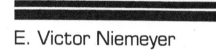

E. Victor Niemeyer

Garland Publishing, Inc.
New York & London, 1984

Library of Congress Cataloging in Publication Data

Niemeyer, E. Victor (Eberhardt Victor), 1947–
    The effect of energy supply on economic growth.

    (Outstanding dissertations in economics)
    Originally presented as the author's thesis (Ph.D.)—
University of Texas at Austin, 1976.
    Bibliography: p.
    1. Economic development—Mathematical models.
2. Energy consumption—Mathematical models.
I. Title. II. Series.
HD75.5.N53 1984   338.9'0724   79-7940
ISBN 0-8240-4188-7

All volumes in this series are printed on acid-free,
250-year-life paper.

Printed in the United States of America

THE EFFECT OF ENERGY SUPPLY

ON ECONOMIC GROWTH

by

EBERHARDT VICTOR NIEMEYER, III, A.B.

DISSERTATION

Presented to the Faculty of the Graduate School of

The University of Texas at Austin

in Partial Fulfillment

of the Requirements

for the Degree of

DOCTOR OF PHILOSOPHY

THE UNIVERSITY OF TEXAS AT AUSTIN

December 1976

Acknowledgments

This dissertation could not have been completed without the assistance of many individuals. The thanks and acknowledgment that I would like to give them here is small repayment for the help, advice and encouragement that I have received.

Michael Kennedy, the chairman of my dissertation committee, deserves special thanks. He was instrumental in both the development of the approach to the topic that was used and in the implementation of that approach in the model. Working closely with me throughout the research, his guidance helped me to avoid many pitfalls in developing the model, and his patience and encouragement made working with him a real pleasure. In the writing of this dissertation I benefited greatly from his editorial assistance as well as his ability to spot a run-on-sentence. His knowledge, insight and enthusiasm in economic theory not only guided me in the completion of the dissertation but re-awakened my appreciation of the theory as well. For all of these things I am grateful.

Stephen L. McDonald, James W. McKie and James L. Weatherby, Jr., the other members of my dissertation committee, deserve thanks for their advice and comments which helped me to correct many errors of both content and presentation in the dissertation. I am grateful for their assistance as well.

The Center for Energy Studies provided financial support throughout my work. Without their support this work would not have been possible.

Most of all, special thanks go to my wife, "Charlie," for her help in typing the many drafts, for her invaluable editorial assistance, and most of all, for keeping me from becoming discouraged when progress was slow. Her joy upon the completion of this dissertation may even surpass my own.

TABLE OF CONTENTS

I.   Introduction   1

II.   Recent Literature on Energy and   9
      Economic Growth

      Higher Oil Prices and the World Economy . .   10
      FEA, Project Independence Report   11
      The Price of Energy and Potential   13
        Growth of Developed Countries
      U.S. Energy Policy and Economic   17
        Growth, 1975-2000
      An Aggregate Model of Energy and   25
        Economic Growth

III. Structure of the Model   29

      I.   Introduction   29
      II.   Static Structure   31
      III. Dynamics of the Model   40
      IV.   Energy Supply   43
      V.   Summary   49

IV.   The Sector Allocation of Investment   52

V.   Results and Conclusions   86

      Numerical Assumptions   87
      Results   96
      Conclusions 103

APPENDIX A 109

APPENDIX B 119

References 128

CHAPTER ONE

Introduction

This thesis describes the structure of a multi-sectoral, general equilibrium growth model of the U.S. economy that gives special attention to the energy sectors and presents results from the simulation of this model under varying conditions of energy supply.

A major characteristic of the U.S. economy has been its growth in real output. From 1900 to 1970 real production increased at an annual rate of 3.3%, amounting to a nine fold increase. During the same period per capita output grew at a rate of 1.8%. The benefits of this growth are obvious. It brought great benefits in the form of higher material living standards for people throughout the income distribution. There is now increasing concern that it cannot continue.

One example of the expression of this fear is in a recent article by Robert L. Heilbroner, "Middle-Class Myths, Middle-Class Realities," [23, p. 41] which states,

> But growth is a process whose days are numbered, partly because of a shortage of resources, partly because of pollution dangers. Probably within our lifetime, certainly within that of our children, growth will have to be throttled back.

In the neo-classical theory of economic growth, the rate of growth in output is the sum of the rates of growth of labor input and labor productivity. This result is based on constant costs in production. The problem is that some sectors of the economy experience increasing costs of production, namely, those which fashion primary products from depletable resources. The issue is the effect of rising costs in the production of some commodities important for economic activity on growth. To study this problem an analytical framework is needed that will incorporate the effect of increasing costs in some sectors at the microeconomic level on the process of aggregate economic growth.

In the study of this problem, the interactions between sectors in the supply of intermediate inputs to each other as well as their mutual competition in the factor market necessitates a general equilibrium context. That the competition for some factors such as capital take place over many time periods necessitates a dynamic context as well. The framework developed here can be used to study the impact of increasing costs in individual sectors on aggregate growth, or to study the effects of bottle-necks in particular sectors on aggregate supply.

When discussing a change in conditions of energy supply it is important to distinguish between changes in the supply of international and domestic energy. The action by OPEC has shifted upward the supply curve of energy obtained in international markets. In the domestic energy market, however, the basic supply relationship has not changed. Unless there are barriers to trade, the price of energy in domestic and international markets must be the same, and the change in the world price of energy has forced domestic production up along the pre-existing domestic supply curve so that the marginal cost of domestic energy is equal to the world price of energy.

Between 1951 and 1973, real GNP in the U.S. grew at an annual rate of 3.5%. Employment grew at 1.6% during the same period implying a rate of increase in productivity per worker of 1.9%. Energy has been available throughout this period at declining real prices; between 1950 and 1970 total use of energy in the U.S. increased from 34.1 quads (quadrillion Btus) to 68.8 quads, an annual rate of growth of 3.6%. With the oil embargo and the quadrupling of oil prices by OPEC in 1973, the assurance of supply and the long term decline in energy prices stopped. Because energy use is pervasive in economic activity, the effect of this change in the energy situation on the economy is an important issue.

While the primary goal of this thesis is to analyze the effect of energy supply on economic growth, it also presents a new methodology for approaching this kind of problem. The tool of analysis is a general equilibrium growth model. While theoretical multisectoral general equilibrium growth models have been developed before, this is the first empirically oriented model with endogenously determined non-malleable capital stocks. The sectoral composition by industry closely mirrors the U.S. economy as does the breakdown of final demand into consumption, investment, government, and net exports. The dynamic relationships allocating capital among the different sectors are empirically determined.

Because this model is empirically oriented it must address the solution of nonlinear general equilibrium systems. An algorithm for solving such models is presented in an appendix for chapter 3.

It should be noted that this analysis is general and not limited to the study of energy and economic growth. The same approach can be used to model the effect of changes in the supply of any produced raw material on economic growth.

We now describe the model and some of its features. At the microeconomic level the model solves for market clearing prices for nine produced goods, labor and the market clearing quasi rents for nine sector-specific capital stocks. The nine produced goods are:

1. agriculture, mining and construction

2. manufacturing

3. transportation

4. services

5. coal mining

6. oil and natural gas production

7. petroleum refining

8. electric utilities

9. gas utilities.

These are the sectors used by Hudson and Jorgenson in their study, "U.S. Energy Policy and Economic Growth, 1975-2000," [28]. The first four sectors can be classified as non-energy material goods and services, and the remaining five are energy goods. The nine separate capital goods in the factor market must be distinguished because of the assumption of non-malleability of capital. Once investment in the capital stock of a particular industry has taken place it cannot be moved to provide productive services to some other industry. While the allocation of the capital stock between sectors is fixed, the allocation of labor between sectors can change. In the short run, there are diminishing returns to labor inputs for all sectors.

Prices of the produced goods are equal to their unit costs, which equal the sum of the unit value added and unit intermediate input costs. Intermediate input requirements are determined through an interindustry input-output system. Income is equal to the value added which is equal to total expenditure. Total expenditure is allocated between consumption, investment, government, and net export spending. The simultaneous solution of these features satisfy conditions for general equilibrium.

The dynamic aspect of the model allocates new capital to the different industries on the basis of their individual demands for capital. Technical progress is of the autonomous Harrod-neutral variety. The rate of growth of the effective labor force, which is the sum of the rates of growth of physical units of labor and the rate of growth in labor productivity, is exogenous to the model. Energy supply enters the model through effects on the production functions for domestic energy and through the payment of produced goods to foreigners in exchange for imported oil.

When the conditions governing supply of a commodity deteriorate the price of the commodity will rise. A market economy can be expected to respond to the increased price in four ways. First, the increase in price will cause the prices of the goods that it is used to manufacture to rise and thus discourage their use and motivate final consumers to find substitutes that use less of the scarce commodity. Second, producers trying to maximize profits will attempt

to minimize use of the scarce commodity in production.
Third, profitability of producing the scarce commodity
will rise, inducing more resources to be devoted to its
production. Fourth, more effort will be devoted to developing new processes and techniques that will facilitate
the first three responses over time.

Clearly, the fourth response, technical innovation,
is the most difficult to predict or to model. The response
of consumers and producers is also difficult to measure
in a detailed model. For these reasons the model developed
here concentrates on the third response, the devotion of
more resources to the production of the scarce commodity.
The model assumes that there will be little price induced
substitution by consumers and producers. To the extent
that there is substitution, the model will over-estimate
the effects of scarcity. Over long periods of time neither
these substitution responses nor the technical change
response can be ignored. For this reason this model concentrates on the intermediate term effects on growth.

It should be emphasized that this model, like all
growth models, is essentially a supply model. There is no
monetary sector, so that prices are in relative terms with
the wage rate as the numeraire. It is assumed that monetary and fiscal policy will maintain adequate aggregate
demand so that real output will be equal to potential GNP.

Chapter 2 surveys the recent literature on energy and economic growth. In chapter 3 the analytical model is presented. The dynamic aspect of the model depends on the investment function developed and estimated in chapter 4. Chapter 5 presents the numerical assumptions and the simulation results.

CHAPTER TWO

Recent Literature on Energy
and Economic Growth

· This chapter provides a brief survey of the
literature on models relating energy scarcity and economic
growth. The major recent contributions to this area of
study have been: (1) Edward R. Fried and Charles L.
Schultze, Higher Oil Prices and the World Economy [19];
(2) Federal Energy Administration, Project Independence
Report, 1974 [20]; (3) J.W. Gunning, M. Osterrieth,
J. Waelbroeck of the World Bank, The Price of Energy and
Potential Growth of Developed Countries, An Attempt at
Quantification [22]; (4) Edward A. Hudson and Dale W.
Jorgenson, U.S. Energy Policy and Economic Growth, 1975-
2000 [28]; (5) Esteban Hnyilicza, An Aggregate Model of
Energy and Economic Growth [25].

These studies can be divided into demand studies
and supply studies. The first two papers reviewed are
principally concerned with the impact of energy conditions
on aggregate demand; the third paper is principally a
demand study but it does have some supply elements, and
the last two models reviewed are principally supply
models.

Higher Oil Prices and the World Economy

Higher Oil Prices and the World Economy, the
Adjustment Problem, [19], is principally concerned with
the short term effects of the late 1973 quadrupling of
oil prices by OPEC. In this analysis the short run effects
are caused by deficiencies in aggregate demand coming from
four sources: higher import prices that increase the flow
of import spending; gloomy consumer and investor expectations that reduce those components of aggregate demand;
anti-inflationary monetary policy, and reduced exports
to other oil importing countries.

> In the long run the higher prices of
> energy products will be paid by a real
> transfer of resources--by exports of
> goods and services to the oil producing
> countries and by larger amounts of
> capital and labor devoted to explora-
> tion and development of lowergrade
> domestic fuels. [19, p. 43]

No attempt is made to quantify the long run loss from the
higher real costs, but reference is made to two studies
that do address this issue, OECD, Energy Prospects to 1985,
[37], and Federal Energy Administration, Project Independence Report [20]. These studies estimate that the
decrease in living standards that occur in 1980 in the U.S.,
Western Europe and Japan as a result of moving from $3 to
$10 oil are 1.3%, 2.6% and 4.5% respectively. The Brookings

report also references a World Bank Study that estimates
the effect of a $5 increase in the price of oil on the
rate of growth of the OECD countries between 1973 and 1985
at between .1% and .2%. These studies do not consider
the transition loss due to sharply higher prices. These
transition costs are the

> frictional losses, (that) are inevitable
> as resources are transferred to new
> patterns of production... In the course
> of time these losses diminish substantially
> and eventually disappear, since both capi-
> tal and labor are quite mobile in the long
> run, but in the interim--and quite apart
> from short-falls in aggregate demand--there
> are transition costs not captured by any
> of our measures. [19, p. 54-5]

In summary, Fried and Schulze see three costs of higher oil
prices. These are the initial loss due to lower aggregate
demand, a transition or frictional cost as the economy
changes its structure, and finally, a permanent loss as a
result of the greater real transfer of resources to foreign
producers in return for imported energy.

FEA, Project Independence Report

The FEA Project Independence report, November 1974,
[20] discusses the effects of higher oil prices on economic
growth in its chapter VI, Economic and Social Impacts.
This work compares the impact of different government
policies and different price scenarios on consumption of

energy and on GNP. The government policies considered are accelerated supply of energy, conservation of energy, both, and neither; the price scenarios are $11 and $7 crude. The results are based on a forecasting system that links an input-output table with a long term macroeconometric fore-casting model. The former is presented in Clopper Almon, Jr., et al., 1985 Interindustry Forecasts of the American Economy [1], and the latter is part of the Chase Econo-metric macroeconomic model. The results of these fore-casts presented below are from Table VI-2, p. 320 of the report.

Annual Rate of Growth of GNP

	$11/bbl-Base case	$7/bbl-Base case
1973-77	2.4	4.3
1973-80	2.8	3.8
1973-85	3.2	3.7

The FEA study presents different rates of growth in worker productivity as well as rates of GNP growth, but these appear not to be the result of any independent assessment of changes in worker productivity but, instead, a residual calculated as the difference between the rate of GNP growth and employment growth. In other words, the productivity figures are expost instead of ex ante.

Average Annual Rate of Change in Worker
Productivity

	$11/bbl-Base case	$7/bbl-Base case
1973-77	.5	2.4
1973-80	1.1	2.1
1973-85	1.7	2.2

While the effect of changes in energy prices can
influence aggregate demand it is our feeling that well con-
ducted monetary and fiscal policy can counter these problems;
our concern is with the effect of changes in energy supply
on the economy's capacity to provide goods and services.
The following study, while still essentially a demand study,
begins to address the problem of the effect of energy supply
conditions on growth of potential GNP.

The Price of Energy and Potential Growth
of Developed Countries

This paper by Gunning, Osterrieth and Waelbroeck
(GOW) [22], presents a model that analyzes several possible
effects of higher oil prices on the economies of developed
countries. The paper begins with a theoretical analysis
of the effect of higher energy prices on the level of
production, investment productivity, and the useful life
of capital goods, as well as the potential mitigation of
these effects by the import of capital from oil producers.

The theoretical analysis is applied in a simulation model
of developed countries of the world called IBRD SIMRICH
OECD in order to quantify the effects of higher energy
prices. Only the basic analytical framework, a general
outline of SIMRICH, and the results from SIMRICH will be
reported here.

The analysis of the impact of energy prices on the
level of production is similar to the effect-of-a-tariff
analysis in international trade. GOW assume the economy
produces two goods, energy and other goods, with diminishing returns for any factor, but with constant returns
to scale in all factors. Energy needs intermediate input
of material for its production, and material production
similarly requires energy. Consequently, higher prices
for energy mean that more materials must be expended to
both import and produce domestic energy, leaving a smaller
net product. In the GOW analysis, whether this short term
static welfare loss shrinks or grows over time depends
on the effect of higher energy prices on the productivity
of investment, the useful life of the capital stock, and
the potential imports of capital from oil producers.

Total investment should decline, due to lower
savings resulting from the loss of income discussed above.
However, average investment productivity for the economy,
which is just an average of productivity in material and

energy production weighted by the relative magnitude of
investment flows, could rise if the increase in average
productivity of investment in energy production were
large enough to offset the decrease in average productivity of investment in materials production. The principal
shortcoming in this analysis is that it takes the allocation of investment between the two sectors as fixed,
when one would expect the flow of investment in a market
economy to respond to changes in relative productivities.

Capital imports from oil producers can mitigate
the effects of higher energy prices on the economy that
were mentioned earlier. In real terms, the cost of the
imported oil is the amount exported to the oil producers.
Because the oil producers have a limited capacity to
import they invest their surpluses until the time when
their import capacity increases. The surplus should be
treated as a net loan from abroad and subtracted from investment in the definition of GNP. However, most of the
inflow of funds does not go directly towards the purchase
of equity, but is banked, and hence subject to a "banker's
gain," the gain from investing funds at a higher rate of
interest than that at which they were borrowed.

Of the four effects of higher energy prices
mentioned, the analysis of the effect on the level of
production and the discussion of capital imports seem the

most useful. The major shortcoming of the analysis of the
changing rate of productivity of investment is that it ig-
nores the profit seeking dynamics of investment allocation
between sectors. The analysis of the effects of importa-
tion of capital from oil producers is useful in that it
illustrates the flaw in looking at the balance of trade
with oil producers for one year in isolation.

The SIMRICH OECD model has the previously described
analysis embedded in its 38 equations and identities. The
model has an elaborate dynamic structure, but very little
sectoral detail. The dynamic structure is exemplified in
the production equations that consider the pattern of past
investment. The lack of sectoral detail shows up, for
example, in the consumption sector, where only aggregate
consumption as a function of aggregate GNP is analyzed.
In essence, the model is a dynamic two sector model with
more detail at the macroeconomic-financial level than at
the micro level.

The model was simulated under two oil price scenarios, a constant price of $3.21/barrel and a price of $8.19
(the 1975 price in 1973 dollars). The short run response
of production to higher energy prices is a reduction in
domestic product of $44.8 billion or about 1.48%; if prices
do not adjust rapidly the loss becomes an extra $1 billion.
The long term response to higher oil prices is equally

small. The rate of growth of real national income from
1973 to 1985 drops from 4.8% to 4.7%. Higher oil prices
are found to actually increase the useful life of capital
slightly, but to cut the rate of growth of value added per
unit of capital from 3.86% to 3.59%. Finally, the bankers'
gain by any of three different measures is found to be
about 30 billion in 1985; i.e., GNP in the OECD countries
ends up being higher by that amount if surpluses are re-
invested in the OECD countries.

U.S. Energy Policy and Economic Growth, 1975-2000

We next describe the Hudson-Jorgenson (H-J) model
presented in the Bell Journal, Autumn 1974 [28]. This
model is an important step in the study of the relationship
between energy scarcity and economic growth. Its strong
point is the empirical microeconomic detail it brings to
the issue, while its principal shortcoming is the lack of
interaction between the micro and macroeconomic levels of
the model. The model is composed of several submodels.
These submodels are a macroeconometric growth model, a
model of consumer behavior, a model of producer behavior
and a model of interindustry transactions. A discussion
of these submodels and a description of how they inter-
relate will now be given.

The macroeconometric growth model determines the rate of economic growth in the overall economy. In it, the allocation of production between consumption and investment and the distribution of income between capital and labor are determined through a production possibility frontier relating these aggregates. The prices of the two primary inputs as well as the values of final demand and its components are determined for use in the other submodels. It is in the macroeconometric growth submodel that different assumptions about tax rates influence the rate of economic growth.

In the model of producer behavior unit cost functions for nine industrial sectors are used to determine the set of nine product prices in each year. The price of each of the nine produced goods is a function of the prices of all nine produced goods, the prices of capital and labor services that are provided by the macroeconometric growth model, and the price of competitive imports, which is exogenous. Given the prices of the primary inputs and imports, prices are determined by the simultaneous solution of the price equations.

This model of producer behavior is based on duality theory, which we will now discuss further. The production function relates levels of output of a product to the amounts of inputs employed in its production; its dual, the cost function, relates the cost of production to the prices of the inputs and the quantity to be produced. Shepard [39] demonstrated that the cost function and the production function can equally well represent a production technology. In addition, the cost function has a useful property: its partial derivatives with respect to prices of the inputs are the input demand functions.

Let $C = C(y,P)$, where y is the scalar quantity of output and P is the vector of the input prices. Then the quantity of inputs demanded, x_i for input i, is equal to $\partial C(y,P)/\partial P_i$. A simple proof of this proposition can be found in Diewert [11, p. 495]. For the case of constant returns to scale, the unit input demand functions are the partial derivatives of the unit cost functions. Unit input demand functions are equivalent to input output coefficients; i.e.,

$$\partial C_i(P)/\partial P_i = x_{ij} \equiv a_{ij},$$

where a_{ij} is the amount of the ith input necessary for production of one unit of the jth good.

Samuelson's Non Substitution Theorem shows that with constant-returns-to-scale, prices are independent of the composition of final demand. Therefore, once we have obtained the simultaneous solution of the cost functions, the input output matrix, composed of the a_{ij}, is

determined for all possible final demand vectors. The
H-J model marks a sharp improvement in the state of I-O
models by including price dependent input-output coefficients.

The consumer behavior model uses the nine prices
derived by the model of producer behavior and the value
of total consumption spending provided by the macroeconometric growth model to determine the quantities of consumption purchases of the output of each of the nine
sectors. It accomplishes this through the use of an
indirect utility function. The functional form used,
log linear, implies that the budget share of each commodity
is fixed. This implies unitary price and income elasticities of demand for each commodity.

The model of interindustry transactions is based on
input-output analysis, with the fundamental modification
that the interindustry and primary input coefficients
are endogenous to the submodel, depending on relative
prices. The cost functions estimated in the model of producer behavior and the prices derived from the simultaneous
solution of the cost functions are used to derive input-
output and primary input demand coefficients as indicated
above. The price vector is also used, in conjunction with
the final demand figures the macroeconometric growth model
derived for government, investment and export spending,

to fill out the final demand vectors. Once final demand levels and the interindustry transactions matrix have been obtained, levels of gross output in each sector can be calculated. The amounts of the primary inputs necessary to produce these levels of gross output are finally calculated. This completes the solution of the H-J model.

Figure 1 helps demonstrate the relationships among the different submodels. It is important to note that flows are one way only, and that no pair of models exchange information, either directly or indirectly.

There are three principal weaknesses of the H-J model. The first is due to the one-way flows of information, or the hierarchical nature of the model. The prices of capital, labor, and imports are exogenous to the models of producer behavior and interindustry transactions, and there is no assurance that the demands for capital and labor services and imports derived from the interindustry model will equal the supplies of these factors assumed in the macro growth model. The value of total productive services demanded will equal the value of total productive services supplied, but there is no guarantee that the quantity demanded of each individual factor will equal its availability. In effect, there are no constraints on the total use of capital and labor services at the microeconomic level. The macro model employs constraints that factor

Figure 1

The Flow of Information in the
Hudson-Jorgenson Model

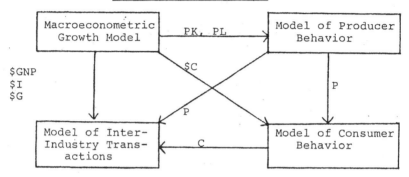

PK   price of capital services

PL   price of labor

$C   dollar value of total consumption

P   vector of product prices

C   vector of consumer spending (by sector)

$G   dollar value of government purchased

$GNP   dollar value of GNP

$I   dollar value of investment spending

supply equal factor demand in its determination of $GNP,
PK, and PL, but there exists no assurance that these
constraints will be preserved in the model of interindustry
transactions.

This shortcoming has been remedied in latter work
in which consistency between the macro model (MM) and the
interindustry model (IM) demands for factor inputs is
achieved.

> In order to achieve consistency between
> the MM and the IM, iteration on the amount
> of capital services and value of net ex-
> ports is required. The two models predict
> values for these independently of each
> other. Two exogenous inputs into the MM
> and IM need to be varied, and thereby en-
> dogenized, until consistency is achieved.
> (DRI Computer User's Manual for the
> Generalized Interindustry Transactions
> Model, p. 2 [10])

This modification in the model presented in the
Bell Journal is one conceptual improvement on the growth
model. But the treatment of capital in this model still
has difficulties. The most important is the malleable
nature of capital in the model. If capital is malleable,
then capital services as well as labor can flow freely
between sectors in the short run. This means that each
sector experiences constant returns in the short run,
which negates the possibility of sectoral bottlenecks.
This removes much of the basis for sectoral detail in the

model. If the capital stock for each sector is fixed, each
sector experiences increasing costs in the short run due to
diminishing returns to the variable inputs. Only a model
with this feature can realistically represent the effect
of supply bottlenecks on aggregate growth.

There are further problems in the H-J model's
treatment of energy supply. The first problem is that
domestic production does not experience endogenously increasing costs with depletion of reserves. The model can
have exogenously increasing costs in any sector due to the
exogenous nature of the technical change parameter used in
the cost functions, but such a formulation would be independent of domestic production. A second problem is that
in the H-J model the amount of imports of oil is independent
of both foreign prices and domestic production capibilities.
This model cannot adequately represent the relationship
between world oil market conditions, domestic market conditions, and economic growth.

In summary, the H-J model is deficient as a growth
model because it requires no consistency between supply
and demand for factor services (in its earlier formulation)
and because it has constant returns in the short run due to
the assumed malleable nature of capital services. It is
deficient as an energy model because domestic production
does not face increasing costs due to depletion and

because the influence of foreign supply conditions is not
properly represented in the model. In other words, the
H-J model already assumes what we are interested in
determining.

An Aggregate Model of Energy and Economic Growth

The model discussed here is presented in a M.I.T.
Energy Laboratory Working Paper that was presented at the
Third World Congress of the Econometric Society in Toronto,
Canada, August 1975 [25]. This model is a two sector model
of the U.S. economy that is closely related to the H-J
model. While not as detailed, the Hnyilicza model presents
several major conceptual advances over the H-J model in its
treatment of capital and production structure.

The major improvement in this model is that the
capital stock is not malleable, which leads to diminishing
returns in the short run. This model also has a more
elaborate production structure in which the two sectors
each have joint production of their respective outputs
distinguished on the basis of destination of output. This
means that the energy sector produces energy for consumption and energy as an intermediate input as two joint
products. Like the H-J model, the Hnyilicza model employs
translogrithmic cost functions in the specification of
its production structure (see Christensen, Jorgenson,
and Lau, [8]). There are many advantages to this

specification of cost functions but there are important
disadvantages in this form as well. The most important
for our purposes is that the translog form is a second
order local approximation of the technology; for some
ranges of input prices the cost function may not be convex which implies positively sloped input demand functions.
This means that models employing such structures can break
down when simulating the effects of major shifts in prices
such as those brought on by OPEC.

   While quite an improvement over the H-J models,
this model still has some serious drawbacks. One problem,
a practical problem and not a conceptual one, is the degree
of aggregation. While there are no theoretical reasons
why this model cannot be expanded to any number of sectors,
the practical difficulty in estimating the key relationships in the production and consumption structure of the
model is staggering.

   The non-malleable nature of the capital stocks in
this model is the biggest advance over the H-J model.
With fixed capital, however, comes the problem of allocating investment (derived from saving at the macroeconomic level) to the distinct capital stocks. Hnyilicza's
model allocates investment between the energy and non-energy
capital stocks exogenously. This same problem exists in
the GOW model discussed above, where investment flows are

independent of the different sector productivities of capital. In a market economy, the response of investment flows to relative sectoral demands for capital is an important element in determining the economy's long term response to supply bottlenecks at the individual sector level. Hnyilicza, as well as GOW, ignore this important aspect of the problem of how an economy responds in the long run to changes in energy supply.

Still another problem with the Hnyilicza model is that its treatment of energy supply, both domestic and foreign, is exactly the same as the treatment of H-J. Once again, this means that domestic costs of production do not rise with depletion of reserves and that imports (and their price) are exogenously determined. Neither this model nor the H-J model can adequately model the effect of a change in world market conditions on economic growth.

A model that can adequately represent the impact of changes in energy supply on economic growth must have the following features. Like the H-J model, it must have extensive sectoral detail at the microeconomic level. Like the Hnyilicza model, it must have fixed inplace, non-malleable, capital stocks that imply diminishing returns and increasing costs in the short run. Unlike these two models, a model that can properly assess the impact of changes in energy supply on economic growth must

endogenously allocate investment to the different sector
specific capital stocks. It should also have an energy
supply structure that shows increasing cost with cumulative domestic production due to the depletion of reserves,
and imports of foreign energy should be endogenously
determined in a simultaneous framework that considers both
the price of foreign crude and domestic productive
capability. The analytical framework for such a model
is developed in the next chapter.

CHAPTER THREE

Structure of the Model

I. Introduction

In order to evaluate the impact of energy scarcity
on economic growth, we develop a model that integrates the
effects of changes in the characteristics of energy supply
on economic phenomena at the micro and macroeconomic levels.
Higher energy prices imply that a greater amount of economic resources must be devoted to the acquisition of energy.
If more resources are devoted to producing energy, less
are available for the production of other goods. This
immediately affects the GNP at the macroeconomic level,
which then affects the amount of savings available for investment. These changes in the amount of investment resources available to the economy then affect the economy's
ability to respond to the higher energy prices in following
years through judicious investment. Therefore, the model
must show both the short run response at the macro level
of microeconomic phenomena, and show the long term response
to bottlenecks at the microeconomic level.

A market economy can be expected to work out short
term supply bottlenecks and eventually resume year to year

growth at the balanced rate. However, the eventual re-
sumption of growth from one year to the next at the balanced
rate does not mean that the transition has been costless.
The issue, then, is how much will be lost during the course
of the transition to the new conditions of energy supply.
A measure which shows this loss is the average compound
rate of growth from a base period prior to the change in
energy supply conditions, a rate that we will call the
intermediate term rate of economic growth.

Long term equilibrium requires both the short run
general equilibrium conditions of supply and demand equality in each market, as well as equal rates of profit in all
industries. The rate of growth in the supply and demand of
all commodities and factors of production (except labor)
must be equal to the sum of the rate of growth in the labor
force and the rate of growth in worker productivity. In
the absence of scarcity of energy, the model maintains
equilibrium in both the short run and the long run. When
energy supply conditions change adversely, short run equilibrium is still maintained, but long term equilibrium is
only approached. The economy is simulated by solving the
model for the static equilibrium each year; the dynamics
of the model work through the effect each year's solution
has on the solutions for subsequent years.

The remainder of this chapter discusses the static short run characteristics of this model, its dynamic and long term characteristics, and how conditions of energy supply are modeled.

II. Static Structure

In each year the level of production, net supply, final demand, price, and primary input requirements must be determined for each of the nine industries included in the model. These are:

1. Agriculture, construction and nonfuel mining

2. Manufacturing

3. Transportation

4. Services

5. Coal mining

6. Crude oil and natural gas production

7. Petroleum refining

8. Electric utilities

9. Gas utilities.

This is the nine sector breakdown of economic activity employed by the Hudson-Jorgenson model [28], the source of much of this model's data.

A. Supply

The supply of capital services available to each industry, $\bar{K}_i$, is exogenous in any year and cannot be shifted to other sectors; i.e., the capital stock is fixed in place. Unlike capital services, labor is freely mobile between industries, and only the total amount of labor that can be employed by the economy, $\bar{L}$, is fixed in each year. These considerations lead to the resource constraints

$$\sum_i L_i = \bar{L} \tag{1a}$$

$$K_i = \bar{K}_i \quad i = 1,\ldots 9 \tag{1b}$$

where

L_i - amount of labor employed in the production of good i

K_i - amount of capital services employed in the production of good i.

This can be written in vectors as

$$K_s = \begin{bmatrix} \bar{L} \\ \bar{K}_1 \\ \cdot \\ \cdot \\ \cdot \\ \bar{K}_9 \end{bmatrix} = \bar{K}$$

where K_s is the vector of primary input supply.

Supply of each of the nine produced goods depends on the quantity of labor and capital services employed in their production through the production functions.

$$Q_i = Q_i(L_i, K_i) \qquad i = 1, \ldots 9 \qquad (2)$$

where

Q_i - gross output of good i.

Production requires intermediate inputs of the other produced goods as well as labor and capital services. Each unit of output of good j requires a_{ij} units of good i in its production. The intermediate input requirements per unit of output are shown in the input output matrix,

$$A = \begin{bmatrix} a_{11} & a_{12} & \cdot & \cdot & a_{19} \\ a_{21} & & & & \\ \cdot & & & & \\ \cdot & & & & \\ a_{91} & \cdot & \cdot & \cdot & a_{99} \end{bmatrix} \cdot$$

The supply of net output, Y, is the amount of gross output left over once intermediate input demands have been met. It satisfies the relationship

$$Y = Q - AQ \qquad (3)$$

where Y and Q are nine element vectors of net and gross output respectively.

B. Prices and GNP

The price of any good is equal to its unit cost of production, which can be broken down into the unit cost of intermediate inputs and unit value added.

$$P = A'P + v \qquad \text{or} \qquad \text{(4a)}$$

$$P = (I-A')^{-1}v \qquad \text{(4b)}$$

Here, P is the nine element vector of product prices and v is the 9 element vector of value added for each product.

Now let r be the 10 element vector of factor price,

$$r = \begin{bmatrix} w \\ r_1 \\ \cdot \\ \cdot \\ \cdot \\ r_9 \end{bmatrix}.$$

Here w represents the wage rate and r_i the cost of capital services in sector i. GNP equals the value of factor payments,

$$GNP = r'K_s.$$

Unit value added, v, is defined as

$$v = b'r$$

where b is a 9x10 matrix of unit primary input requirements.

C. Demand for Factors of Production

The production functions are concave and homogeneous of degree one. For any set of factor prices, w and the r_i, unit labor and capital service requirements are determined by profit maximizing behavior. Because nonmalleability of capital implies that there are nine different capital goods, the matrix of unit primary input requirements, b, can be written as,

$$b = \begin{bmatrix} b_{L1} & b_{L2} & \cdots & \cdots & b_{L9} \\ \hline b_{K1} & 0 & & & 0 \\ 0 & b_{K2} & & & \\ 0 & 0 & & & b_{K9} \end{bmatrix}$$

where b_{Li} and b_{Ki} are the respective unit labor and capital service requirements of industry i.

The amount of primary inputs demanded by the economy, K_d, depends on the level of gross output, Q.

$$K_d = bQ \qquad (5)$$

Here K_d is a 10 element vector partitioned as

$$K_d = \begin{bmatrix} L \\ \hline K_1 \\ \vdots \\ K_9 \end{bmatrix}$$

L is total labor demand and K_i is capital services demanded by sector i.

D. Demand for Net Output

The quantity of net output demanded depends on
prices and GNP. Walras' Law guarantees that

$$GNP = P'Y_d \qquad (6)$$

where Y_d is a nine element vector of net output demanded
by the economy. Y_d may be broken down into five components,

$$Y_d = C + I + G + X - M \qquad (7)$$

where C, I, G, X, and M are the nine element vectors of
real consumption, investment, government, export and import
spending.

The total values of investment and government
purchases are the constant percentages, s and t, of GNP,
and the total value of consumption is equal to the residual
percentage, 1-s-t, of GNP.

$$P'I = s \; GNP \qquad (8a)$$
$$P'G = t \; GNP \qquad (8b)$$
$$P'C = (1-s-t) \; GNP \qquad (8c)$$

Consumers are assumed to maximize a Leontief utility
function. They thus purchase the produced goods in fixed
proportions.

$$C_i = \frac{(1-s-t)\ GNP}{\Sigma \phi_j P_j}\ \phi_i \qquad (9)$$

Here C_i is real consumption spending on good i, and ϕ_i is the amount of good i in the unit consumption bundle. The ϕ_i sum to unity.

Real investment and government spending are similarly determined in equations 10 and 11.

$$I_i = \frac{sGNP}{\Sigma \theta_i P_i}\ \theta_i \qquad (10)$$

$$G_i = \frac{tGNP}{\Sigma \psi_i P_i}\ \psi_i \qquad (11)$$

Here I_i and G_i are the real purchases of sector i's output by investors and the government respectively, while θ_i and ψ_i are the amounts of sector i's output in the unit bundles of investment and government goods.

It should be noted that these demand functions allow no substitution in response to changes in relative prices. This restrictive functional form is a worst case assumption.

Exports are assumed to be exogenous each year.

$$X_i = \bar{X}_i \qquad i = 1,\ldots 9 \qquad (12)$$

Here X_i is the amount of real export spending on the output of sector i.

Imports are purchased in fixed proportion bundles with weight γ_i for sector i. The total value of imports is assumed equal to the value of exports, leading to the following import demand functions.

$$M_i = \frac{P'X}{\Sigma \gamma_i P_i} \gamma_i \qquad i = 1,\ldots 9 \qquad (13)$$

Here M_i is real spending on imports of the good produced by sector i. The vector with elements M_i is M.

In each year, solving the model involves finding the set of prices, P and r, at which supply equals demand for all commodities in the product and factor markets. Because product prices are a function of factor prices and the price of labor is the numeraire, the solution of the model only requires determining the set of factor prices at which the demand for capital services equals the supply.

E. Mathematical Summary of Static Model

Supply

Factors of Production

$$K_s = \overline{K}$$

Gross output

$$Q_i = Q_i(L_i, \overline{K}_i) \qquad i = 1,\ldots 9$$

Net output

$$Y_s = Q - AQ$$

Prices and GNP

$$P = A'P + b'r \quad \text{or}$$

$$P = (I-A')^{-1} b'r$$

$$GNP = r'K_s$$

Demand

Factors

$b = b(r)$ Unit primary intput requirements are a
            function of factor price

$$K_d = bQ_s$$

Gross output

$$Q_d = (I-A)^{-1} Y_d$$

Net output

$$Y_d = C + I + G + X - M$$

$$C = C(GNP,P)$$

$$I = I(GNP,P)$$

$$G = G(GNP,P)$$

$$X = \overline{X}$$

$$M = M(\overline{X},P)$$

Equilibrium Requirements

$$K_s = K_d$$

$$Q_s = Q_d$$

$$Y_s = Y_d$$

$$GNP = P'Y = r'K_s$$

III. Dynamics of the Model

A. Growth of Capital

The dynamic element of the model is allocation of investment for increases in the sector specific capital stocks. After the static model has been solved in any year, there exists a stock of total investment goods that have been produced in that year. The problem is then how to allocate investment in order to build up the nine different capital stocks. As noted above, once investment goods have been installed for producing a particular type of output they cannot be shifted to produce other goods. Sectoral composition of the capital stock by origin is assumed to be the same for each industry, i.e., each industry's capital stock is assumed to contain identical proportions of the nine produced goods.

The allocation of investment goods among the different industries is assumed to be done on the basis of expected profitability, π^*. Profits, π, are defined as total revenue minus variable costs of production.

$$\pi_i = P_i Q_i - Q_i \sum_j a_{ji} P_j - wL_i \qquad i = 1,\ldots 9 \qquad (14)$$

Let D_i be the real amount of investment goods to be added to the capital stock of sector i. Then,

$$D_i = D(\pi_i^*) \quad i = 1,\ldots 9 \qquad (15)$$

However, equation (15) is not unconstrained, since the total amount of real investment goods allocated must be equal to the total amount available.

$$\sum_i D_i = \frac{sGNP}{\sum_j P_i \theta_i} \qquad (16)$$

Chapter 4 discusses the estimation and functional form of equation 15.

The capital services available to a sector in any year, $\overline{K}_i$, is a constant fraction, k, of the capital stock, S_i, available to that sector.

$$\overline{K}_i = kS_i \quad i = 1,\ldots 9 \qquad (17)$$

Capital stocks of all sectors are assumed to depreciate at a constant annual rate, d, so that

$$S_i^+ = (1-d) \, S_i + D_i \quad i = 1,\ldots 9 \qquad (18)$$

where S_i^+ is the following year's capital stock. This then determines the following year's availability of capital services.

B.   Growth in Labor

The rate of growth of labor supply, g, as well as the rate of growth of Harrod neutral technical progress, v, is exogenous to this model.

$$\overline{L}^+ = (1+g)\ \overline{L} \qquad (19)$$

$$v = \overline{v} \qquad (20)$$

Here $\overline{L}^+$ is next year's supply of labor. v, the rate of Harrod neutral technical progress, is assumed to be the same in all industries. The rate of growth of the economy depends on the two rates of growth, g and v. It should be noted that v measures the rate of change in technical knowledge, not the ex post change in output per unit of labor input.

C. Long Run Equilibrium

Barring short term disturbances, the model outlined here would grow at the constant rate of growth g + v, and would have the characteristics of long run steady state growth as outlined by Solow, Growth Theory [40, p. 2]. There are four characteristics that exemplify steady state growth:

(1) real output per unit of labor grows at a constant rate, v;

(2) the capital stock grows at a constant rate exceeding the rate of growth of labor input;

(3) the capital stock and total output grow at the same rate, i.e., the capital-output ratio is constant; and

(4) the rate of profit for capital remains constant. The rate of growth of output per unit of labor is
v, the rate of growth of labor input is g, and capital and
total output grow at rate g + v. These rates of growth
will not necessarily prevail in the short run when the
environment in which the economy operates changes.

IV. Energy Supply

While the model has five different energy sectors,
only two of them, coal mining and oil and natural gas
production, actually produce energy, while the other
three either convert energy into different forms or dis-
tribute it to users. Due to the large amount of coal
resources available, long run diminishing returns in its
production does not become a problem. Oil and natural
gas production in the U.S. is experiencing long term
diminishing returns, however, and the analysis concentrates
on the supply of this energy source.

The supply of energy from crude oil and natural gas
comes from two sources which must be treated separately,
foreign markets and domestic production. Foreign oil
is assumed to be supplied by a cartel. It sets a real
price for oil in terms of the prices of other commodities,
and then ships as much oil as its customers desire in
return for commodities at that price. In this model the
cartel is assumed to purchase manufactured goods with the

revenues from oil sales. Let P_O and P_M be the prices of oil and manufactured goods, and let q be the cartel price. The supply curve for cartel oil is shown in Figure 2. This supply curve has infinite elasticity at price q.

Imports of oil and exports of manufactured goods to the cartel are represented in the vectors M_c and X_c. M_c is a vector of zeros except for the sixth element, m_o, which represents imports of oil. X_c is a nine element vector of zeros except for the second element x_m, which represents exports of manufactured goods to the cartel. m_o is determined from the cartel oil supply function, 21.

$$m_o = f\left(P_O / P_m, \ q \right) \qquad (21)$$

The assumption of a balance of trade with the cartel,

$$P'X_c = P'M_c,$$

allows the calculation of x_m in equation 22.

$$x_m = P_O \cdot m_o / P_m \qquad (22)$$

When the import and export vectors, M_c and X_c, are added to the import and export vectors, 12 and 13, foreign oil markets are incorporated into the model through net output demand equation 7.

The production of domestic oil and natural gas is assumed to require more and more primary inputs as

Figure 2

The Supply Curve of Oil by the Cartel

cumulative production increases. This is modeled by
adding a Hicks neutral efficiency parameter, γ, to the
production function for oil.

$$Q_6 = \frac{1}{\gamma} Q_6 (L_6, K_6) \qquad (23)$$

As γ increases it takes more labor and capital
services to get a unit of oil. The level of γ is assumed
to depend on cumulative production of oil and gas. γ
should not be expected to increase indefinitely, however.
As cumulative domestic production increases γ will eventually rise so high due to depletion of reserves that
non-traditional ways of obtaining oil will become profitable. Examples of alternate methods of obtaining oil
are coal liquifaction and oil from oil shale and tar
sands. The alternate sources have the common characteristic that they are expected to be in very elastic
supply once the price of oil reaches their threshold cost
of production. This threshold unit cost of production,
say B, which puts an upper limit on γ, is called the
backstop cost, and the technology which it corresponds
to is the backstop source of oil.

Let, for example, coal liquifaction and gasification be the backstop source of oil, and assume that
it requires five times as much capital and labor to
produce a barrel of oil by this method than by current

practice. Once production of oil by standard techniques
reaches the point where it takes five times as much labor
and capital as it does now to produce a barrel of oil,
further production will be with coal liquifaction and
gasification. The relevant backstop technology need not
be coal transformation, of course.

The rate of growth of γ depends on the level of
the backstop and the rate at which it is being approached.

$$\gamma = \min\left(\left[\frac{AC}{TR}\right]B + 1, B\right) \tag{24}$$

Here B is the assumed backstop value of γ, TR is total
reserves available before the backstop cost becomes
relevant, and AC is cumulative domestic production of oil.

In this model of depletion there is no consideration of the discrepancy between price and marginal cost
based on the finite nature of domestic reserves that was
proposed by Hotelling [26]. This phenomenon is due to
the choice that producers have in the temporal allocation
of production. In the Hotelling model the relationship
between the return to current production and the return
to production in the following time period for every
pair of time periods is governed by equation 25,

$$r(P_t - MC_t) = P_{t+1} - P_t \tag{25}$$

where r is the rate of interest, P_t is the price of the
resource in time period t and MC_t is marginal cost of
production in period t based on cumulated production until
then. If relationship 25 holds for every pair of time
periods, producers will be indifferent as to when they
produce a unit of output, while if equation (25) does
not hold for a pair of time periods it would be profitable
to shift production between them until (25) is satisfied.
This gives the most efficient temporal distribution of
production.

This analysis applies to a closed economy in
which the price of oil is endogenous. However, in the
model outlined here, the real price of oil is determined
exogenously by the foreign cartel. If the real cartel
price remains constant over time, equation 25 will hold
only if domestic production increases in each period to
a rate at which marginal cost is equal to the cartel price.
In other words, if the real price is externally determined
and is unchanging, there are no returns to reducing
current production and holding out for higher prices in
the following time period.

If the real price, as determined by the cartel,
were going to rise, sometime in the future it would be
profitable for domestic producers to hold back current
production and wait for the price increase. Unfortunately,

the economic model that has been outlined in this chapter
is unable to consider such price expectations. This
deficiency in the model is tantamount to a worst case
assumption, because consideration of expected price changes
would lead to a more efficient temporal allocation of
production and thus a higher rate of growth.

This concludes the discussion of the energy sectors. Next, we will present a brief description of
how the model responds to changes in conditions of energy
supply.

V. Summary

A good way to illustrate how the model works is to
trace the effect of a change in energy supply conditions.
In this section we first discuss the effect of a change
in foreign energy supply conditions, an increase in the
cartel price of oil. Then we discuss the effect of domestic oil resource depletion on the economy.

An increase in the cartel price of oil means that
more manufactured goods must be exported to pay for the
imported oil, leaving less available for domestic use.
The price for the services of capital goods that produce
oil is then bid up, and this increases the unit cost of
domestic oil to the cartel price. The higher price of oil
reduces domestic demand for final output through the income

effect of higher prices (as no substitution is allowed).
The higher price of capital services in oil production
induces producers in that sector to hire more labor which
permits domestic production to increase. Increased
domestic production of oil plus curtailed demand due to
the higher prices help relieve the excess demand for oil.
The economy shifts labor, with diminishing returns, into
the production of domestic oil, and into   manufactured
goods which are exchanged for oil with the cartel at the
new, less favorable, terms. The additional labor needed
to produce oil, directly and indirectly, can no longer
produce other commodities, and real output is less than
it would have been had there been no increase in the
cartel price for oil.

Profitability for manufacturing and oil production are higher and capital formation takes place faster
in these sectors than in others. In the next year the
economy will have more capital to produce manufactured
goods to obtain foreign oil, and more capital in place
for producing domestic oil, but will have less capital
to produce other commodities.

When the conditions of oil production deteriorate
due to depletion of domestic reserves, the effect in each
year is that more labor must be devoted to the production

of oil if output is to be maintained. In addition, the existing capital stock in the oil producing sector has become less productive, and profits are lower. Therefore, less new investment is devoted to capital formation for oil production. In any given year output is lower due to depletion, and over time less capital is directed to oil production as well. It is, instead, directed to manufacturing for the purchase of imported oil. If the conditions under which the cartel supplies oil are un- changed there is little long term loss to the economy other than the accelerated depreciation of its existing capital in oil production. If the cartel raises the price, the economy bears a higher real loss because of the reduced ability to substitute domestic oil for foreign.

It should be noted that the above descriptions are partial equilibrium analyses. The model considers the interactions between markets in a fully simultaneous general equilibrium solution. Only such a model can completely assess the impact of changes in energy supply conditions on economic growth.

CHAPTER FOUR

The Sector Allocation of Investment

In the model outlined in Chapter 3, the capital
stock available to each sector is fixed in the short run.
In this chapter we theoretically develop and estimate
the relationship that allocates each year's net investment among the different sector-specific capital stocks.
In the following sections we review the recent empirical
investment literature, describe the investment model we
will be estimating, describe the data base used, and discuss how the results apply to the growth model.

How quickly a market economy responds to a change
in the conditions of energy supply, and thus returns to
long run equilibrium, depends on how fast it rechannels
resources to those sectors experiencing an increase in
demand. In the short run this means directing more variable
inputs such as labor and intermediate goods (with diminishing returns) into those sectors, while in the long run
fixed input of capital is directed into those sectors
as well.

The response in the short run depends on assumptions about the mobility of variable inputs and the

elasticity of substitution of these inputs with capital
in the production function. In this time period, the
capital stock available to any sector is fixed. However,
over time the amount of capital depends on the rate of
new additions (gross investment) minus retirements
(depreciation). If retirements are proportional to the
capital stock, we have

$$K_i^+ = (1-\delta)\ K_i + I_i \tag{1}$$

where K_i^+ is capital stock available to sector i in the
next time period, δ is the rate of depreciation, K_i is
the capital stock of sector i in the current time period
and I_i is gross investment in the capital stock of sector i.
For a given rate of depreciation, δ_i, the change in a
sector's capital stock depends on the amount of investment,
I_i.

There are two distinct approaches to the problem
of allocation of investment among the different sectors'
capital stocks. One is the portfolio analysis approach
that considers the problem of choosing among investments
at different expected rates of return; the other considers
the demand for capital based on the firm's optimization
of its net worth over time. The portfolio approach has
the advantage that it is consistent with profit maximization
at the macroeconomic level. In this approach, new

capital would be allocated to those sectors with the greatest expected returns, with adjustment for risk.

The demand for capital stock approach, though based on intertemporal profit maximizing behavior, is a partial equilibrium solution to a general equilibrium problem. In this approach there is no assurance that the sum of desired investment by the individual firms will equal aggregate saving. (A difference between desired investment and total saving is important to a Keynesian macroeconometric model, but such a difference has no role in a growth model.) Despite this fundamental shortcoming, other aspects of the demand for capital approach make it the best point for beginning our discussion. The partial equilibrium solutions can be scaled up or down to satisfy general equilibrium constraints. Investment processes have complex time structures due to the time necessary to develop and confirm expectations in the decision making process, and due to the lags in implementation of investment decisions. The existing literature on investment at the industry level has explored the time structure of the investment process in detail. Finally, the role of uncertainty can cloud the impact of individual sector rates of return in a portfolio model.

The most appropriate point of departure in a survey of the recent literature on investment is the Jorgenson

survey article in the 1972 Journal of Economic Literature
[31]. In this article Jorgenson surveys the use of flexible accelerator models of investment at both the individual
firm and industry level. The industry level studies are
most relevant for our purposes. The major contributions
to the empirical literature on investment at the industry
level surveyed were Anderson [3,4]; Bourneuf [6]; Eisner [14,
15, 16]; Evans [18]; Hickman [24]; Jorgenson and Stephenson
[35]; Meyer and Glauber [36]; and Resek [38]. We will
examine three of these models in developing a foundation
for our own model of investment.

Since 1963 the literature has focused on the deter-
minants of gross investment, the structure of replacement
investment, and the time structure of the investment
process. (The integration of anticipatory data, from the
McGraw Hill Survey, into investment equations has also
been discussed;* but this issue is not useful for our
purposes.) Our discussion will focus on the studies most
useful in the development and estimation of our investment
model, those of Jorgenson, Eisner and Hickman.

Jorgenson has developed the best theoretical basis
for his investment model, as well as the most complex lag

---

*Principally by Jorgenson [24] and Eisner [15, 17].

structure. The model is presented in two articles by
Jorgenson [29, 30] and in an article that was co-authored
with Stephenson [35]. The model is based on Irving Fisher's
neoclassical theory of optimal capital accumulation. In
Jorgenson's models firms maximize their present value,
which is the discounted value of future revenues minus
expenses for inputs on both current and capital account.
The firm's production function is well behaved; i.e.,
it is twice differentiable, with positive marginal rates
of substitution between inputs and positive marginal
productivities of inputs, and is strictly convex. The
production function can be written

$$F(Q, L, K) = 0. \qquad (2)$$

Here Q, L, and K are output, labor and capital services.
Additions to the capital stock are determined by the
relation

$$\dot{K} = I - \delta K. \qquad (3)$$

Net investment equals gross investment, I, minus depreciation, δK. Net revenue, R, is defined by the relation

$$R = pQ - sL - qI. \qquad (4)$$

Here p, s, and q are the prices of output, labor inputs,
and investment goods. The present value of the firm is
defined by

$$V = \int_{0}^{\infty} e^{-rt}(R-D)\,dt \qquad (5)$$

Here r is the rate of discount and D is the firm's tax
liability. The maximization of (5) subject to (2) and (3)
yields the marginal productivity conditions

$$\frac{\partial Q}{\partial L} = \frac{W}{P} \qquad (6a)$$

$$\frac{\partial Q}{\partial K} = \frac{C}{P} \; . \qquad (6b)$$

Here W is the cost of labor inputs and C is a measure of
the user cost of capital. The measure C is determined by
the price of capital goods, the rates of interest and
depreciation, and the tax structure.

If firms could acquire capital stock as quickly as
they hire labor services, the marginal productivity conditions could be solved simultaneously to obtain the optimal
amounts of labor and investment. Of course, the actual
level of capital available to a firm may differ from the
optimal level due to the time necessary to complete investment projects. Jorgenson's model assumes a sequential
process in which the firm first solves for the desired
level of production and labor input given the existing
capital stock, and then uses these levels of output and
labor input to determine the desired level of capital
using the marginal productivity condition (6b).

Calculated in this manner, the desired amount of capital (which will determine the amount of investment that the firm will plan) will not be equal to the optimum level of capital. Jorgenson states, however, "with stationary market conditions, such a process is easily seen to converge to the desired level of net worth." [30, pg. 249]

If firms use this sequential method of investment planning, the desired level of capital is determined (assuming, for simplicity, a Cobb Douglas production function) by

$$K^* = \beta \frac{PQ}{C}. \tag{7}$$

Here P and C are the product price and the user cost of capital, and β is the elasticity of output with respect to capital in the Cobb Douglas production function

$$Q = L^\alpha K^\beta \qquad \alpha+\beta < 1. \tag{8}$$

Using the assumption that firms will initiate new investment projects until the existing level of capital plus the backlog of uncompleted projects equals the desired level of capital, the Jorgenson-Stephenson (J-S) model postulates

$$I_t^E = \mu(S) \left[K_t^* - K_{t-1}^* \right]. \tag{9}$$

Here the I_t^E is investment for expansion of capital (as opposed to replacement), and

$$\mu(S) = \mu_0 + \mu_1 S + \mu_2 S^2 + \dots .$$

Here μ_i are weight coefficients and S is a lag operator defined by $S^n x_t = x_{t-n}$. Replacement investment is a fixed proportion, δ, of the existing capital stock. $\mu(S)$ is assumed to have a rational generating function, so that

$$\left[I_t - \delta K_t\right] = \frac{\gamma(S)}{\omega(S)} \left[K_t^* - K_{t-1}^*\right] . \qquad (10)$$

Here $\gamma(S)$ and $\omega(S)$ are polynomials of the lag operator, S, and their ratio is finite approximation of $\mu(S)$. Equation (10) can be written in a stochastic specification as

$$\left[I_t - \delta K_t\right] = \sum_{j=0}^{m} \gamma_j \left[K_{t-j}^* - K_{t-j-1}^*\right]$$
$$+ \sum_{j=1}^{n} \omega_j \left[I_{t-j} - \delta K_{t-j}\right] + \varepsilon_t \qquad (11)$$

A definition of desired capital is needed in order to estimate equation (11). Such a definition is provided by specifying the variables in equation (7). Q_t, P_t, and C_t are the value added, the product price and the user cost of capital in time period t. The elasticity of output with respect to capital, β, cannot be estimated separately from the coefficients, γ, in equation (11); therefore, the regression coefficients are estimates of βγ.

Jorgenson and Stephenson limit the order of the polynomial ω(S) to two, and the order of the polynomial γ(S) to seven, with the latter having at most four non-zero elements. According to Jorgenson [32], the principal advantage of using a rational generating function for μ is that it allows the finite approximation of any lag distribution. The principal shortcoming, as with other lag structures such as Almon's [2], is that some a priori specification of the term of the lags is needed. With no theoretical constraints on the length and complexity of the lag, J-S try a variety and pick the structure that minimizes the estimated standard error of the regression, consequently biasing the standard error of the estimate and thus the standard errors of the coefficients downward. [35, pg. 182]

The J-S model (equation 11) was estimated with quarterly data for fifteen manufacturing sub-industries and three manufacturing aggregates (total, durables, and non-durables), for the time period 1947 to 1960. Eighteen separate equations were therefore estimated with time series data. The equations generally fit well, having R^2's ranging from .45 to .96, with only two equations

having R^2 less than .80. The coefficients were generally
significant.

Because Eisner has contributed extensively to the
empirical literature on investment it is difficult to specify a single investment model that characterizes his work.
Eisner's 1960 Econometrica article, "A Distributed Lag
Investment Function," [13] best describes the theoretical
basis of his work. Changes in a firm's level of sales
(and profits), if they are permanent as opposed to transitory, will require changes in the firm's desired level of
capital stock. Eisner's model postulates that the relationship between current sales, current profits and current
investment, i.e., the simple flexible accelerator model,
will be weak both because changes in these variables can
be considered transitory, and because there are lags
between the decision to invest and its implementation.
As Eisner put it,

> ...we have in mind a world of risk and un-
> certainty in which business firms strive
> to maximize the mathematical expectation
> of some monotonic increasing function of
> expected future profit, subject to a pro-
> duction function with decreasing marginal
> returns to each factor and positive cross
> partial derivatives. This means, in
> particular, that for a firm initially in
> equilibrium it pays to increase the stock
> of capital for permanent of certainly ex-
> pected increases in demand for output.
> (Eisner [13], p. 1)

Eisner tests his theory with the same type of tests
used in testing Friedman's permanent income hypothesis.
Changes in sales can be thought of as having two components,
a transitory component and a permanent component. Changes
in sales within industry groups are assumed to be transitory, while changes in sales between groups are assumed to
reflect permanent changes. Regressions of investment on
changes in sales for within industry groups have much
lower coefficients than regressions of group means between
groups, and this result supports Eisner's permanent income
theory of investment.

In this investment theory, a change in permanent
sales, ΔS_t, will lead to a determinate change in the desired
capital stock, ΔK_t^*. This holds exactly only if the elasticity of substitution between capital and labor is zero,
or if the price of output and the prices of factors of production remain unchanged. For the case in which product
or factor prices change for a non-zero elasticity of substitution, the inclusion of a profits variable captures
the effect of these changes on the desired capital output
ratio [17, p. 97].

Due to an adaptive expectations mechanism and the
time lags in implementation of investment decisions, a
change in permanent sales, ΔS_t, will have the following
effect on net investment in future time periods.

$$\Delta F_t^i + \Delta F_{t+1}^i + \Delta F_{t+2}^i \cdots = \Delta K_t^* \qquad (12)$$

Here F_h^i is the change in capital stock in time period h due to the change in sales in time period i, and K_t^* is the change in the desired capital stock. We have the further relation

$$\Delta F_{t-j}^i = \beta_j \Delta S_i . \qquad (13)$$

Net investment then becomes

$$I_t - R_t = \Delta F_t^t + \Delta F_t^{t-1} + \Delta F_t^{t-2} + \cdots$$

$$\qquad (14)$$

$$= \beta_0 \Delta S_t + \beta_1 \Delta S_{t-1} + \beta_2 \Delta S_{t-2} + \cdots$$

Here I_t and R_t are gross investment and replacement investment in time period t.

Though this is the basic theory, Eisner does not estimate any equations in this form. Changes in sales are deflated by the level of sales for a particular year, and gross investment is divided by the capital stock. Some of Eisner's models include the level of profits, while others do not. In short, there is no single equation that Eisner seems to favor.

In a study comparing four investment models, Jorgenson, Hunter and Nadiri [33], use the following representation of Eisner's model.

$$I_t = \beta_0 + \beta_1 \Delta S_{t-1} + \beta_2 \Delta S_{t-2} + \beta_3 \Delta P_{t-1}$$

$$+ \beta_4 \Delta P_{t-2} + \beta_5 I_{t-1} + \beta_6 K_t \qquad (15)$$

Here ΔS and ΔP are changes in sales and changes in profits before taxes. The lag structure is a modified Koyck distribution, with the first time period weight flexible, and further weights declining geometrically. This lag structure has the disadvantage of closely constraining the form of the lag, but it does not require the comparison of different specifications on the basis of standard errors of estimate.

Most of Eisner's work used McGraw-Hill investment data for both individual firms and industries. Equations were estimated in time series, cross section, and pooled cross section and time series form. They generally show that sales are very important in determining investment, and that profits are most important in determining the timing of investment. Firms in both high and low profit sectors of the economy tend to invest more rapidly in response to a rise in profits in the recent past.

The Jorgenson, Hunter and Nadiri article compared the estimates of four different investment models based on a common set of data for individual manufacturing industries. The four models were Anderson [3], Meyer-Glauber [36], Eisner [13, 15, 16] and Jorgenson-Stephenson [35].

The results of a goodness of fit comparison based on the
standard error of the regressions for fifteen different
manufacturing industries showed the Eisner and Jorgenson-
Stephenson models clearly superior. The Eisner model had
a better fit than the Anderson model for all fifteen
industries, and a better fit than the Meyer-Glauber model
in thirteen out of fifteen cases. The Jorgenson-Stephenson
model was superior to both the Anderson and Meyer-Glauber
models in fourteen cases. The Jorgenson-Stephenson model
fit better than the Eisner model in eleven cases. Because
the four models were estimated on a different set of data
than that for which they were originally estimated, this
study guards against getting good fits through data mining
in specifying the functional relationships.

In another study done by Jorgenson, Hunter and
Nadiri [34], the four models were compared on the basis of
predictive performance in two tests. One test compared
the errors for a period of prediction with the errors for
a period of fit, and the other test tested the equations
estimated for both time periods for structural change.
The results of this study ranked the Eisner and Jogenson-
Stephenson models (in that order) above the other two.
The authors concluded that the goodness of fit of these
models is "not exaggerated by data mining," and that

the goodness of fit of these models is a "valid indication
of predictive performance" [34, p. 223].

The two investment models that we have discussed
were estimated on quarterly data. Because the growth model
outlined in chapter 3 is an annual model, the investment
equation we will estimate will be based on annual data.
In the Jorgenson survey article on investment two annual
models are presented, those of Bourneuf [6] and Hickman [24].
The model we will estimate is similar to the Hickman model
in some of the variables, and uses Hickman's estimated
capital stocks as benchmarks. The Bourneuf model is inap-
propriate for our use due to its inconsistent treatment
of capital stock and replacement investment. [31, pp. 1138-
9]

The Hickman investment model is a modification of
the standard accelerator model. In the standard accelerator
model net investment is a function of the difference between
last time period's capital stock, K_t, and the desired level
of capital, K_t^*.

$$K_t - K_{t-1} = b(K_t^* - K_{t-1}) \qquad (16)$$

Hickman's modification of this model postulates that the
percentage change in the capital stock is a function of
the percentage gap between the existing level and the desired level of the capital stock.

$$\frac{K_t}{K_{t-1}} = \left(\frac{K_t^*}{K_{t-1}}\right)^b \qquad 0 < b \le 1 \qquad (17)$$

Logarithmically, this can be written

$$\ln K_t - \ln K_{t-1} = b(\ln K_t^* - \ln K_{t-1}). \qquad (18)$$

The desired stock of capital is a logarithmic linear function of the expected long term level of output, Y_t^*, the expected relative price of capital goods, P_t^*, and a trend variable, T.

$$\ln K_t^* = \ln a_1 + a_2 \ln Y_t^* + a_3 \ln P_t^* + a_4 T. \qquad (19)$$

The expected levels of output, Y_t^*, and prices, P_t^*, are functions of the present and past levels of output and prices, respectively.

$$a_2 \ln Y_t^* = a_{21} \ln Y_t + a_{22} \ln Y_{t-1} \qquad (20)$$

$$a_3 \ln P_t^* = a_{31} \ln P_t + a_{32} \ln P_{t-1} \qquad (21)$$

This procedure modifies Koyck's; it postulates a constant speed of adjustment of desired capital stock, but uses a weighted average of current and recent levels of output and relative prices.

Equations (20) and (21) can be substituted into equation (19), which can then be substituted into equation

(18) to get the equation

$$\ln K_t - \ln K_{t-1} = b[\ln a_1 + a_{21}\ln Y_t + a_{22}\ln Y_{t-1}$$
$$+ a_{31}\ln P_t + a_{32}\ln P_{t-1} + a_4 T] \quad (22)$$
$$- b\ln K_{t-1}.$$

In Hickman's equations, the variable T^2 is present for some
industries to allow for non-linear net trend. The time
trend variables are included to measure the effects of technical change on capital requirements. The validity of
having a time trend variable depends on the nature of technical progress assumed. In models that include technical
change in the form of increases in labor effectiveness time
trend variables have no place in investment equations.
Also, including time trend variables presents the following
problem.

> In addition to technical progress, they
> may reflect to an unknown extent the
> effects of scale economies, price induced
> factor substitution, compositional shifts
> in capital requirements, and changes in
> the ratio of value added to total value
> product. ([24], p. 64)

The Hickman model has the potential strength of an
a priori specification of the lag structure (as does the
Eisner model, but not the J-S model), but Hickman varies

the number of lagged independent variables for different industries in order to improve the statistical fit. The principal contribution of Hickman's work from out point of view is that it estimates an annual model, and that it provides data sources for benchmark capital stocks and depreciation rates.

As we have seen, of the three investment models surveyed, the J-S model has the most rigorous theoretical development. However, there is a basic weakness to this theory which will now be discussed. The problem arises in the definition of desired capital stock, which is derived from the sequential solution of the marginal productivity equations (6a) and (6b).

As mentioned earlier, J-S assume that firms act on the basis of a sequential rather than a simultaneous solution to the marginal productivity conditions. Firms are assumed to first determine the optimum level of output given the existing level of capital, and then to use that level of output to determine the desired level of capital. If the J-S model assumed that firms wished to employ the optimum level of capital derived from a simultaneous solution of the marginal productivity conditions, instead of using the sequential process, then current levels of output would not enter into the determination of the desired level of capital.

Whether firms use an iterative process, or directly solve for the optimum, when determining the desired level of capital stock, is crucial for the validity of the theoretical foundation of J-S's investment equations. Borch [7, p. 372] suggested that

> It is natural to assume that intelligent management will see more than one step ahead in this process and try to optimize output level and capital stock simultaneously. This seems particularly natural under the perfect certainty assumed by Professor Jorgenson.

This criticism would not be important, however, if the iterative process converged rapidly.

In order to test the rate of convergence an experiment was designed based on the Cobb-Douglas production function described above. The parameters assumed were

$$P = 5$$
$$C = 2$$
$$W = 3$$
$$\alpha = .74$$
$$\beta = .25$$

The optimal value for capital derived from simultaneous solution to the marginal productivity conditions in this case is 27.1. The iterative process was started with a level of capital 10% higher than optimum, 29.8. After 20 iterations the desired level of capital had converged to

28.0 (3% above the optimum). While these results are illustrative, they do suggest that convergence does not necessarily take place quickly.

The issue of using observed levels of output, sales or profits in determining the desired level of capital is extensively discussed by Gould [21]. Gould sees investment as a process involving two parts: the determination of the desired capital stock, and the adjustment of the stock to this desired level. In the context of the investment equation $I_t = F(K_t^*, K_r)$, the determination of K_t^* is the first part of the problem, and the specification of F is the second. (K_r is the level of capital available to the firms.) Gould's analysis is based on the dependence of output, sales and profits on the availability of capital. If there is no instantaneous adjustment of capital to desired levels, then the relationship described by F constrains output, sales and profits. This reduces the effectiveness of these variables in determining K*.

This work points to the limitations of Jorgenson and Stephenson's iterative process, which uses suboptimal desired levels of capital due to sequential instead of simultaneous solution of the marginal productivity conditions, (6a) and (6b). In the example presented above, a simple lag scheme with a one period adjustment mechanism was used. Gould uses more elaborate lag adjustment mechanisms, and compares time paths of approach to the optimum level of capital derived from using the iterative and the simultaneous solutions to the marginal productivity conditions. Gould shows that using observed levels of output in determining the desired level of capital stock can lead to misspecified investment models that may fit well but fail in prediction.

Finally, Gould recommends that investment models use variables to determine the desired level of capital that are based on information exogenous to the firm, such as product demand and factor supply relationships. This may be the direction to go for future advances in the empirical study of investment, but it is beyond the scope of this work. Jorgenson, Hunter and Nadiri tested the predictive performance of investment models that used output and sales to determine the desired level of capital, and found it to be satisfactory [34]. Gould's critique of the investment models that we have discussed is theoretically valid, but does not have significant impact from an empirical standpoint.

It should be noted that the theoretical weakness in the J-S model only shows up because of the rigorous formulation of the theory. The Eisner and Hickman models make no explicit connection between changes in sales or output and the desired level of capital, yet under certain assumptions the J-S model is very similar to the Eisner model. If the relationship between sales and value added in an industry is stable, and if the product price as well as the user cost of capital remain constant, then the J-S model reduces to the Eisner model without the profit variables [7, p. 270].

An evaluation of the three models discussed above shows that there is no strong, well-developed, theory of investment at the industry level. However, Borch has argued that rigorous theoretical foundations, because they must of necessity be major simplifications of a very complex process (the determination of investment decisions) can be counterproductive and that the ad hoc empirical approach is the most useful [7, p. 273].

For the purposes of the growth model, Eisner's model of investment, as formulated by Jorgenson, Hunter and Nadiri, is a good combination of theoretical foundations and empirical results. Firms invest in order to make profits, which depend on future demand and expenses. Over time, changes in demand are more significant at the industry level than changes in desired capital output ratios, so that the principal determinant of investment is the change in sales. Changes in profits are also important in that they form a "catchall for a number of factors not encompassed in current sales." (Eisner, [17, p. 97]).

Current and past changes in sales and profits determine
expectations about future sales and profits, which determine changes in the desired level of the capital stock.

A straightforward modification of the Eisner model
that could be used in the growth model is

$$I_t - \delta K_t = \beta_0 \Delta Y_t + \beta_1 \Delta Y_{t-1} + \beta_2 \Delta P_t$$
$$+ \beta_3 \Delta P_{t-1} + \beta_4 (I_{t-1} - \delta K_{t-1}) \tag{23}$$

While this equation closely resembles the equation used
by Jorgenson, Hunter and Nadiri to represent Eisner's
investment theory, it is different in four ways.

The first difference is that the independent
variables are lagged by one time period. This is done because the equation is estimated with annual data instead
of quarterly data; the lags appropriate for a quarterly
model are too short for an annual model. The lag structure
corresponds to a Koyck distribution, with flexible coefficients for the independent variables in the first time
period, and with the coefficients declining geometrically
thereafter. While this is not as flexible as the lag
structure used by J-S, it still gives substantial flexibility, especially for an annual model, and does not
require comparing alternate specifications on the basis of
standard errors to determine the lag structure.

The second difference is that this equation explains net as opposed to gross investment. In effect, an equality constraint is imposed on the coefficient of capital in the Eisner model to make it equal to the depreciation rate. This is done because the data series have different depreciation rates for the different industries, while the growth model assumes a uniform depreciation rate for all industries. For this reason, a net investment model is easier to incorporate into the growth model.

In the third place, this equation does not have a constant term. Without a constant term the equation is homogeneous of degree 1, which is a requirement for balanced growth in the growth model.

Finally, Eisner uses changes in sales, while this equation uses changes in output (value added) similar to the J-S and Hickman models. This change was made because of the wider availability of data on output by industry for non-manufacturing industries than of data on sales. Using output instead of sales is also more appropriate when doing a cross-section study of industries because value added is a better measure of output than sales.

The data used in estimating the investment equation is a pool of time series for seven industries, including mining, manufacturing of non-durables, manufacturing of durables, non-rail transportation, rail transportation,

communications, and public utilities. While there is con-
siderable variety in this list of industries, it is not
comprehensive; construction, wholesale and retail trade,
and services were excluded because of lack of investment
data. The industries included accounted for 82% of total
plant and equipment expenditures in 1975.

The investment data was obtained from the plant and
equipment expenditure series in the Survey of Current
Business. Investment figures were deflated by the price
index for non-residential fixed investment. Constant dollar
output by industry was used as the value added figure.
The profit variable was "profit type income" plus net
interest by industry. All of the above variables were
also taken from the Survey of Current Business.

Hickman's book [24] contains historical series on
the capital stock and depreciation rates by industry from
1947 to 1962. The depreciation rates, as well as the
1947 capital stocks, for all the industries in the sample
except mining were derived from this source. Mining was
not in Hickman's sample of industries. We used the
industry total figure for the depreciation rate, and the
benchmark capital stock was inferred using investment,
the assumed rate of depreciation, and the rate of growth
of output.

There are still difficulties in applying equation
(23) to the growth model. These difficulties arise from
the relationships among the capital output ratio, the
parameters of equation (23), and the rate of growth.
The problem can be illustrated with an example that employs
a simplified version of equation (23).

$$I_t = \beta \Delta Y - \lambda I_{t-1} \qquad (24)$$

In long run steady state growth the following
relationships must hold

a) $I_t = (1+g)I_{t-1}$

b) $gY = \Delta Y$

c) $vY = K$

d) $I = \Delta K = gK$

In these equations g is the rate of growth, and
v is the capital output ratio. The first two relationships
can be combined with equation (24) to obtain

$$I = \beta g Y + \frac{\lambda}{1+g} I.$$

This simplifies, with the help of relationship (d), to

$$(1 - \frac{\lambda}{1+g}) gK = \beta g Y.$$

This implies

$$\frac{K}{Y} = v = \frac{\beta}{(1-\frac{\lambda}{1+g})} , \qquad (25)$$

or that for given values of β and λ, the capital output
ratio depends on the rate of growth. This clearly contra-
dicts the result of neoclassical growth theory that the
growth rate is independent of the capital output ratio.

An acceptable modification of equation (23) which
would remedy this problem is to put the variables in
percentage form.

$$\left(\frac{I}{K}\right)_t = \beta_0 \left(\frac{\Delta Y}{Y}\right)_t + \beta_1 \left(\frac{\Delta Y}{Y}\right)_{t-1} + \beta_2 \left(\frac{\Delta P}{P}\right)_{t-1}$$
$$+ \beta_4 \left(\frac{I}{K}\right)_{t-1} \tag{26}$$

Here I, Y, P, and K are net investment, output, level of
profits, and level of capital stock. As long as the average
capital output ratio equals the marginal capital output
ratio (an implication of constant returns along a balanced
growth path), percentage change in output requires the
same percentage change in capital.

In long run steady state growth the following conditions will hold.

$$\left(\frac{I}{K}\right)_t = \left(\frac{\Delta Y}{Y}\right)_t = \left(\frac{\Delta Y}{Y}\right)_{t-1} = \left(\frac{\Delta P}{P}\right)_t = \left(\frac{\Delta P}{P}\right)_{t-1}$$
$$= \left(\frac{I}{K}\right)_{t-1} = g \tag{27}$$

If the parameters to equation (26) are constrained to add
to one, these conditions will be met. This allows one to

estimate one investment equation for all sectors (despite different capital output ratios) in long term steady state growth.

There is still one estimation problem with equation (26). While output of the industries in our data sample is never zero, profits may be zero, which leaves two of the variables in equation (26), $(\frac{\Delta P}{P})_t$ and $(\frac{\Delta P}{P})_{t-1}$, undefined. A solution to this difficulty consistent with long run steady state growth conditions and with long term equilibrium in a market economy is to use the difference between the industry's rate of profit, r_i, and the economy wide rate of profit, r_T.

$$r_i = \frac{P_i}{K_i} \qquad r_T = \frac{\Sigma P}{\Sigma K}$$

In long run equilibrium in a market economy investment flows will eradicate differences in the profitability of different industries. This result, of course, is in accord with the portfolio model of investment determination that was discussed at the beginning of the chapter.

The form of the investment equation used in the growth model is

$$\left(\frac{I}{K}\right)_t = \beta_0 \left(\frac{\Delta Y}{Y}\right)_t + \beta_1 \left(\frac{\Delta Y}{Y}\right)_{t-1} + \beta_2 (r - r_T)_t$$
$$+ \beta_3 (r - r_T)_{t-1} + \beta_4 \left(\frac{I}{K}\right)_{t-1} \qquad (28)$$

All variables are subscripted by industry except r_T which
is the aggregate profit rate. β_0, β_1, and β_4 are constrained to sum to one in order to preserve balanced
growth condition 27. This constraint on equation (28) gives
it the following form when estimated.

$$\left(\frac{I}{K}\right)_t - Z = \beta_0 \left(\left[\frac{\Delta Y}{Y}\right]_t - Z\right) + \beta_1 \left(\left[\frac{\Delta Y}{Y}\right]_{t-1} - Z\right)$$
$$+ \beta_2 (r-r_T)_t + \beta_3 (r-r_T)_{t-1}$$

(29)

where $Z = \left(\frac{I}{K}\right)_{t-1}$ and $\beta_4 = 1 - \beta_0 - \beta_1$.

Equation (29) was estimated using OLS on the set of
pooled cross section and time series data discussed earlier.
The results are presented in Table 1. These results show
that the percentage change in the capital stock is clearly
related to current and past percentage changes in output.
Divergence of an industry's profit rate from the average
appears to have little effect on net investment. The
general fit of the equation (as represented by the R-square
statistic) is significant, and when considering that the
data was a pool of time series and cross section data is
quite reasonable. The percentage nature of the data helps
control for the possibility of heteroscedasticity resulting
from using a cross section.

TABLE 1

Results from the Estimation of Equation 29

(Constraint: $\beta_4 = 1 - \beta_0 - \beta_1$)

Coefficient	t-value
$\beta_0 = .1409$	7.662*
$\beta_1 = .1175$	5.724*
$\beta_2 = -.0212$	-.504
$\beta_3 = .0363$	.858
$\beta_4 = .7416$	(derived)

R-squared = .35   (adjusted for degrees of free-dom)

$F(3.185) = 34.69$

Durbin-Watson d statistic = 1.72

*significant at the 1% level.

The lag structure of the equation takes the form

$$\left(\frac{I}{K}\right)_t = \alpha_1\left(\frac{\Delta Y}{Y}\right)_t + \alpha_2\left(\frac{\Delta Y}{Y}\right)_{t-1} + \alpha_2\lambda\left(\frac{\Delta Y}{Y}\right)_{t-2}$$

$$+ \alpha_2\lambda^2\left(\frac{\Delta Y}{Y}\right)_{t-3} + \dots \tag{30}$$

$$+ \gamma_1(r-r_T)_t + \gamma_2(r-r_T)_{t-1} + \gamma_2\lambda(r-r_T)_{t-2}$$

$$+ \gamma_2\lambda^2(r-r_T)_{t-3} + \dots$$

Here
$$\alpha_1 = \beta_0 = .1409$$

$$\alpha_2 = \beta_0 + \beta_4\beta_0 = .2220$$

$$\gamma_1 = \beta_2 = -.0212$$

$$\gamma_2 = \beta_3 + \beta_4\beta_2 = .0206$$

$$\lambda = \beta_4 = .7416.$$

Given the lack of statistical significance of the estimated coefficients for the profit variables in equation (29), the elaborate lag structure presented in the second line of equation (30) may not be warranted. Equation (29) was reestimated with a zero constraint imposed on β_3, which implies a simple geometrically declining set of weights on the profit variable. The result for this estimation are presented in Table 2.

TABLE 2

Results from the Estimation of Equation 29
(Constraints: $\beta_4 = 1 - \beta_0 - \beta_1$; $\beta_3 = 0$)

Coefficient	t-value
$\beta_0 = .1372$	7.679*
$\beta_1 = .1186$	5.787*
$\beta_2 = .0135$	1.168
$\beta_3 = 0$	(constrained)
$\beta_4 = .7443$	(derived)

R-squared = .35

F(2,186) = 51.74

Durbin-Watson d statistic = 1.73

*significant at the 1% level.

The results presented in Table 2 are little different from those presented in Table 1. The coefficient
on profits is still not significant, but it does have the
theoretically expected positive sign. For this reason
the formulation of equation (29) with β_3 constrained to
equal zero is used in the growth model. The lag structure
for this equation is (using the symbols employed in
equation 30)

$$\alpha_1 = \beta_0 = .1372$$

$$\alpha_2 = \beta_1 + \beta_4\beta_0 = .2255$$

$$\gamma_1 = \beta_2 = .0135$$

$$\gamma_2 = \beta_3 + \beta_4\beta_2 = .0100$$

$$\lambda = \beta_4 = .7443$$

These values of the coefficients were used for the investment equation in the growth model.

It would not be feasible to simply impose the estimated investment equation on the growth model. It is also
necessary to maintain the constraint that total net investment plus total replacement investment equal total savings,

$$\Sigma I_i^N + \Sigma \delta K_i = sGNP. \qquad (31)$$

Here I_i^N, δ and K_i are net investment, the depreciation rate, and the capital stock of sector i, and s is the saving rate.

Let I_i^A be the net investment for sector i resulting from the solution of equation (29). Net investment in sector i in the growth model will then be I_i^N, according to the relations

$$I_i^N = \eta I_i^A \qquad (32)$$

$$\eta = (sGNP - \Sigma \delta K_i)/\Sigma I_i^A. \qquad (33)$$

In other words, the solutions of equation (29) are scaled to satisfy the total net investment constraint (31).

It should be reiterated that our goal is not to measure possible shortfalls in aggregate demand, but to allocate increases in the capital stock to the different sectors. The model of investment presented here mirrors the historical relationships that have explained net investment for different industries in the U.S. economy. This completes our discussion of the endogenous allocation of gross investment to the different sector specific capital stocks in the economy.

CHAPTER FIVE

Results and Conclusions

This chapter presents the results of simulations
of the growth model under different conditions of energy
supply. A comparison of these simulations shows the impact
of energy costs on economic growth in our model. The
simulations also indirectly shed light on the effect of
the supply conditions of any individual good on economic
welfare. The chapter will also describe the numerical
assumptions used in doing the simulations.

We will first comment on why the simulation technique is used. The model presented in chapter 3 represents a complex economy. While the relationships between
some of the variables are simple, the relationships
between other variables are very complex and depend on
simultaneous solutions of the whole model over many time
periods. The relationship between energy supply conditions and economic growth depends on the complex inter-
action of all the variables in the model so that analytical
expressions that relate endogenous variables to exogenous
variables are impossible to derive. Simulation allows
the analysis of these complex relationships in an

internally consistent framework in which all the assumptions must be specifically stated, and in which all the
equilibrium conditions must be met. Simulation allows the
performance of experiments in which parallel simulations
are done with slightly different assumptions about key
variables in order to show the impact of these variables
on the outcome. In this chapter the variables governing
energy supply are varied in order to demonstrate their
relationship to the rest of the economy over time.

Numerical Assumptions

Most of the numerical assumptions were common to
all the simulations; only the assumptions governing energy
supply were varied. The parameters of the model were
chosen to closely approximate the U.S. economy in 1971,
the base year. This year was chosen because it was the
last year for which much of the data on which the parameters were based was available. The main data source,
the Hudson-Jorgenson model [28], and its underlying
data base [27], provided detailed information on interindustry transactions.

The non-energy numerical assumptions are of two
types, corresponding to different levels of the model.
There are macroeconomic assumptions, such as saving and
tax rates, and microeconomic assumptions, concerning

final demand and production functions. These assumptions remain unchanged throughout our simulations.

The macro level assumptions are as follows. The saving rate is 15%, the tax rate is 22%, and the propensity to consume, marginal and average, is 63%. These values are equal to the percentages of these components of GNP in 1971. The labor force grows at an annual rate of 1.0%, and Harrod-neutral technical change occurs in each sector at 2.5% per year. These two assumptions imply a balanced growth path at a rate of 3.5%. The rate of capital depreciation is 10%. These values roughly correspond to recent historical experience. Using round number approximations instead of exact historical experience does not influence the results when different energy supply scenarios are compared, but does facilitate comparisons.

The source of data for the microeconomic assumptions is the set of interindustry transactions tables for 1971 presented in Hudson and Jorgenson [27]. However, some adjustments of this data were necessary. Hudson and Jorgenson treated imports as a primary input into the production process, while in our model imports are considered a substitute for domestic production. In addition, the Hudson-Jorgenson consumption figures include the services of consumer durables, while our definition is the one used

in the national income accounts. The model's parameter
values have been chosen so that equilibrium occurs in
1971 when all prices equal unity. Correspondingly,
quantities in other years are actually values of output
in 1971 prices.

The interindustry transaction flows and the values
of final demand components in the base year appear in
Table 3. The interindustry requirements matrix, A, can
be obtained by dividing the first 9 elements of the first
9 columns of Table 3 by their respective row totals, Q.
With the exception of ρ, the parameters of the CES value
added function for each sector,

$$V = \theta [\delta w^{-\rho} + (1-\delta) r^{-\rho}]^{-\frac{1}{\rho}} ,$$

can be derived from Table 3 as well. The distribution
parameter, δ, is the proportion of wages in value added,
and θ is the proportion of value added in total cost.
The parameter that determines elasticity of substitution
of capital for labor, ρ, is set at -.75. This value was
not estimated, but was selected as a worst case assumption
corresponding to a floor on the short term elasticity of
substitution of -.25. The desirability of using worst
case assumptions will become evident when the results
are discussed. Two other worst case assumptions are the
fixed coefficient final demand functions, and the fixed

TABLE 3

Interindustry Transactions

	1	2	3	4	5	6	7	8	9	C	I	G	X	M	Q
1	16399	35592	1324	17116	16	288	261	724	295	9142	71444	46864	6565	7221	198800
2	41016	238377	2346	47790	447	369	1123	590	236	224294	66784	53823	31999	34213	674973
3	5541	18039	5778	12375	96	351	1207	765	269	15873	3106	3851	6173	5070	68355
4	34698	93567	12697	158650	912	4895	8317	4411	1214	387848	13978	123120	19178	13161	850325
5	9	1726	6	87	633	0	9	1912	3	88	0	28	419	2	4919
6	9	33	0	111	0	1932	13159	0	4637	0	0	0	2	2653	17229
7	3677	4652	2794	4928	34	86	2163	1547	33	15410	0	1395	984	2507	35196
8	140	5044	83	9120	72	162	195	2773	0	10996	0	536	9	137	28993
9	183	3684	162	1761	2	0	467	1255	7019	5796	0	524	70	438	20487
K	45613	74838	13047	245351	823	7380	4552	9760	4457						
L	51513	199429	30117	353035	1884	1767	3745	5265	2323						

coefficient interindustry transaction matrix, A, both of which were discussed in Chapter 3.

Investment is allocated among the nine sectors on the basis of the criteria developed in Chapter 4.

In examining the results we have concentrated on the effects of changes in energy supply after 5, 10 and 15 years. While it is certainly possible to simulate models over a longer time period, the limitations in the assumptions diminish the confidence in the results for later time periods. The assumption of constant coefficients in inter-industry transactions for production, and in the composition of the final demand vectors, becomes less reasonable with time. The time periods that were selected for concentration in our analysis give a good indication of the short and intermediate term effects on growth of varying conditions of energy supply.

The main criterion for comparison of different scenarios is the rate of growth in consumption, which is closely, but not perfectly, correlated with the rate of growth in GNP. The difference is due to the effects of changes in foreign trade patterns on the composition of final demand. Because the pattern of consumption is invariant with respect to changes in relative prices, there is no ambiguity in finding a price index to deflate nominal values in order to make comparisons in real terms.

As discussed in Chapter 3, there are two types of energy supply conditions, those governing trade with foreign producers and those governing domestic production. The variable controlling foreign supply conditions is the real cartel price of oil in terms of manufactured goods, q. If the cartel price, q, goes from 1.0 to 2.0, then two times as many manufactured goods must be exchanged for a unit of foreign produced oil as previously.

The variables controlling domestic oil production are the backstop cost (in terms of value added) of oil production, B, and the amount of oil that can be produced before the backstop cost is reached. The amount is defined by specifying the number of years (T) that base year (1971) production can be maintained before hitting the backstop cost.

Thus, if the backstop cost, B, is 5 and T is 20, then when cumulative domestic production reaches 20 times the base year's production, 5 times as much capital and labor will be needed to produce a unit of oil (for any given ratio of capital to labor prices) as was needed in the base year.

The cartel price, q, was relatively easy to derive for our simulations. It is the real delivered price of OPEC crude, with adjustments made for a gradual decontrol of U.S. prices. We assumed that the price in 1975 dollars will remain at $13.00 into the intermediate run future. The values for the cartel price are presented in Table 4. Oil imports are assumed to be available in infinite quantity at this cartel set price.

Picking values for the backstop is more difficult. What is being measured is the effect of depletion of domestic reserves, and the resulting increases in production costs. While costs are higher for drilling deeper or further offshore, it is difficult to specify precisely the relationship between production one year and increased capital and labor requirements the next. Ultimately, the backstop for domestic production is an alternate source, perhaps coal liquifaction or shale oil production, and the costs of these technologies have not been well established. Since there is no strong evidence that exactly specifies either the backstop level or the amount of resources that are available before a backstop technology must be used for domestic production, two different backstop cost levels were used in the simulations, B = 3 and B = 5.

With increases in cumulated output the cost of additional output rises as producers use up the easily exploited grades of reserves and move on to those more difficult to exploit. This increasing cost is modeled

TABLE 4

Cartel Price of Oil

Year	Dollar Price (1975 $)	Cartel Price Index
1971	4.60	1.0
1972	4.60	1.0
1973	6.90	1.5
1974	9.00	2.0
1975	9.00	2.0
1976	11.00	2.4
1977-on	13.00	2.8

by increasing the term γ, as defined in Chapter 3.* If
the factor γ is 2.5, then 2.5 times as much capital and
labor will be necessary to produce a unit of oil as was
needed in the base year. Eventually γ will rise enough
to make alternate sources of oil, such as coal liquefac-
tion or production from oil shale, competitive. Due to
the large amounts of reserves of coal and oil shale, the
cost of additional production from these sources will
rise much more slowly with cumulated production. The
cost of plentiful alternate sources of oil provide an
upper limit, B, on the escalation of γ, hence the term
backstop. The relationship between cumulative production
and γ is assumed to linear. As was discussed in Chapter 3,
there is no basis for a discrepancy between price and
marginal cost due to the Hotelling phenomenon in this
model as long as the real price of oil determined by the
cartel remains constant. Due to our uncertainty about
the cost levels at which new sources of oil and gas would
become competitive, the level of the backstop, B, is
treated as an experimental parameter in the simulations
presented.

---

*In Chapter 3, the production function for sector 6
(crude oil and natural gas production) was presented
as

$$Q_6 = \frac{1}{\gamma} \, f(K_6, L_6).$$

The application of the backstop model of depletion
is illustrated in Figure 3. The horizontal axis measures
total cumulative production, and the quantity TR refers to
total reserves available at a cost (in value added) below B,
equal to 20 times the base year level of production. The
vertical axis measures γ, the factor by which value added
must be increased to get a unit of production.

Results

Table 5 shows the 5, 10 and 15 year growth rates
in real consumption for different conditions of energy
supply. The case in which there is no cartel action, i.e.,
in which the price of oil in terms of manufactured goods
is unity, and in which the backstop cost, B, is one, corresponds to the balanced growth case. In this case the
economy grows at 3.5% per year.

The cases in which either there is no cartel (q=1),
or in which there is no deterioration in the cost of domestic production of oil with depletion of reserves (B=1),
are similar in that growth is changed very little from the
balanced growth case. In the first case, the cartel does
not set a high price for foreign oil, but the domestic
economy suffers a deterioration in its own ability to produce crude oil. Here, the growth path is very close to
the balanced growth path over the first five year period.

Figure 3

The Relationship Between Primary Input Requirements in Oil
Production and Cumulative Domestic Production

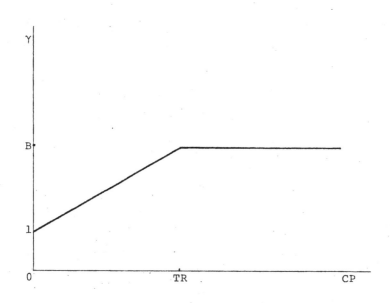

where   γ - factor by which primary input requirements are
              increased

        B - upper limit on γ determined by the backstop
              technology

        CP - cumulative production of oil

        TR - total reserves, equal to 20 times domestic
              production in the base year.

TABLE 5

Average Annual Rates of Growth of
Real Consumption

Cartel Pricing (q)	Backstop Level (B)		
	1	3	5
After 5 years			
No (q = 1)	3.52	3.43	3.34
Yes (q = 2.4)	3.38	3.08	2.93
difference*	-.14	-.35	-.41
After 10 years			
No (q = 1)	3.52	3.45	3.38
Yes (q = 2.8)	3.54	3.11	3.00
difference*	+.02	-.34	-.38
After 15 years			
No (q = 1)	3.52	3.46	3.42
Yes (q = 2.8)	3.61	3.19	3.11
difference*	+.09	-.27	-.31

*The change in the growth rate due to cartel pricing.

In this time the economy is in the process of adjusting to the change in energy supply conditions. Total production becomes more intensive in manufacturing in accord with the principle of comparative advantage. In the long run, domestic crude production shuts down and the economy returns to a balanced growth path, exporting manufactured goods for oil. This can be seen in Table 5 where the rate of growth (for no cartel and B = 5) increases with time from 3.34 to 3.42 as the economy becomes more intensive in manufacturing.

If there is no domestic deterioration in oil production conditions due to depletion of reserves, but the cartel raises its price, a different phenomenon occurs. The economy produces its own energy at a lower opportunity cost in terms of manufactured goods than that available abroad. In this case the economy eventually becomes an exporter of oil and surpasses the balanced growth path. Of course, the oil exporting cartel would have difficulty maintaining a high oil price in the face of exports by the U.S.

Of the two adverse changes in energy supply conditions, a deterioration in the economy's ability to produce crude implies a more pronounced reduction in growth. This is because existing capital in the crude oil sector becomes less productive, and this shock is repeated with

each year. Alternatively, a one time increase in the
cartel price in the face of unchanging domestic production
conditions causes a one time shock that gives the economy
a much higher return to domestic production of crude, a
phenomenon that the economy takes advantage of in the long
run.

The current feeling of vulnerability to foreign
energy sources, of course, stems from a belief that domestic
energy production cannot be substantially increased at
historical costs. The combined effect of higher foreign
energy prices and domestic cost increases (associated with
$B = 3$ and $B = 5$) are presented in Table 5. The worst case,
cartel pricing with $B = 5$, leads to a 2.9% growth rate for
real consumption in the first five years, 3.0% after ten
years, and 3.1% after fifteen years.

Due to the experimental nature of the backstop
parameter, B, the results should be viewed as showing the
effect on economic growth of cartel pricing of foreign
crude for any given set of assumptions on the conditions
of domestic production. As the effects of domestic
depletion become more severe, the effect of cartel pricing
increases, but in all cases the effect is modest. In the
worst case for the 15 year period (B = 5), the effect of
cartel pricing is to reduce the rate of growth of
consumption by .31 percentage points. This means that

consumption in the fifteenth year is 4.6% lower than it
would have been if the cartel had not raised the price of
crude. The corresponding effects of cartel pricing on the
level of consumption after 5 and 10 years are 2.0% and 3.8%
respectively.

Three observations concerning these results are in
order. First, the impacts on intermediate run growth seem
to be quite modest given the large cost increases. This is
basically due to the small role that crude petroleum plays
in the economy as a whole, even at current higher prices.
Second, short run decrements in consumption may well be
overstated in the case of higher foreign prices, since
foreign producers, due to absorptive capacity constraints,
may be willing to accept financial claims in return for
energy imports. Finally, it should be pointed out that
these are worst case simulations with regard to the assumptions made about price elasticities in demand and production, as well as those made about the elasticity of substitution between capital and labor.

Another interesting aspect of the simulations is
the volume of crude oil imported under various scenarios.
Table 6 shows the amount of oil imports (in billions of
1971 dollars), five, ten and fifteen years after the base
year for the different energy supply conditions that have
been discussed.

TABLE 6

Imports of Oil

Cartel Pricing (q)	Backstop Level (B)		
	1	3	5
After 5 years			
No (q = 1)	3.2 (-.94)	11.6 (-.32)	12.7 (-.07)
Yes (q = 2.4)	1.4	8.9	11.9
After 10 years			
No (q = 1)	3.8	18.1 (-.20)	20.8 (-.09)
Yes (q = 2.8)	-6.8	14.9	19.1
After 15 years			
No (q = 1)	4.5	26.0 (-.22)	27.9 (-.09)
Yes (q = 2.8)	-32.6	21.0	25.6

(Numbers in parentheses are the arc price elasticities of imports.)

If B = 1, the response of imports to an increase in foreign oil prices is very elastic. After five years the arc price elasticity is -.94, and after ten years the economy begins exporting oil. As the backstop increases the price response of imports decreases markedly, to arc elasticities of -.32 and -.07 after five years for B = 3 and B = 5 respectively. Thus, import demand becomes less elastic as resource depletion becomes more severe.

While different assumptions about the rate of increase in cost of producing domestic oil do not make much difference in the rate of growth in consumption (as can be seen in Table 5), the different assumptions about depletion have a relatively large quantitative impact on the level of imports when the price of foreign oil is high (as can be seen in Table 6). This issue can only be resolved once the long term domestic oil supply curve is known.

Conclusions

Our overall optimistic findings require a note of caution. The results of the simulations showing that the effect of higher real prices of energy on growth is slight are based on the assumptions underlying the model. Some of the assumptions are numerical, and for these assumptions the worst case has been assumed. There is another assumption that is fundamental, however, which is that the economy will behave as a market economy, with mobile labor resources and prices unconstrained by controls. To the extent that the U.S. economy does not meet these assumptions, the model will understate the impact on growth.

In Chapter 2, five different models of the effect of energy supply on economic activity were discussed. The first two studies that were discussed were principally concerned with the impact of energy supply on aggregate demand and, therefore, their results are not directly comparable to the results of this study. The last two studies reviewed, the Hudson-Jorgenson and Hnyilicza models, do not present any results linking conditions of energy supply to the rate of economic growth. Hudson-Jorgenson apply their model's translog cost structure to the study of substitution of different forms of energy in production and to the possible effects of a BTU tax; they do not make any projections of the effect of varying conditions of energy supply on economic growth. The Hnyilicza paper also presents no results linking different conditions of energy supply and economic growth.

The only study discussed in Chapter 2 that does present results which can be compared to the results presented here is the study done by Gunning, Osterrieth and Waelbroeck using the SIMRICH model. The principal difficulty with their study is the lack of sectoral detail in the production structure. It is clear neither these results were derived in a general equilibrium framework, nor what the relative effects are of the impact on aggregate demand the the impact on potential supply. Therefore, the results of this study cannot be used to assess the effect of varying conditions of energy supply on intermediate term economic growth.

In Chapter 2 we argued that a model that can properly assess the impact of changes in the conditions of energy supply on economic growth must have the following characteristics. It must have extensive sectoral detail at the microeconomic level. It must have fixed, non-malleable capital stocks, which imply diminishing returns in the short run. It must further allocate investment to these sector specific capital stocks endogenously. The energy supply structure should show increasing cost with cumulative domestic production due to the depletion of reserves, and imports of foreign energy should be endogenously determined in a simultaneous framework that considers both the price of foreign crude and domestic productive capability. In this thesis a model with all of these characteristics has been developed and simulated. These simulations show that despite restrictive assumptions about substitution of produced goods in production and

consumption, intermediate term economic growth is relatively insensitive to higher real energy prices.

That an increase in the real price of energy is not
very detrimental to economic growth has many implications.
One is that policies that will increase the price of energy
in order to accomplish some other goal, such as independence from foreign suppliers, will not have major adverse
effects on growth. Another is that increased efficiency
in the use of energy is not essential to coping with higher
energy prices; of course, increased efficiency in use can
be significant in decreasing dependence on foreign sources
of energy. Still another issue for which our results have
implications has to do with the effect of meeting increased standards of environmental quality; i.e., the
effect on growth of more expensive energy conversion
techniques which are less damaging to the environment
are small.

The importance of this study is that its results
have been derived from a general equilibrium analysis that
considers all the important interactions between energy
supply and economic growth. Part of the basis for our
findings is essentially that energy production and
distribution plays a relatively small part in total economic activity. If energy becomes more expensive, more
resources must be devoted to its acquisition, and this

exacts an opportunity cost, but this cost, while possibly very large in absolute terms, is small in relative terms. A casual analysis of the energy sectors of the economy would show that they are a relatively small part of the economy, but that would not be enough to infer that the effect of an increase in the price of energy would be small. Such a limited analysis would not consider the interactions between sectors in production, nor would it consider the longer term interactions between sector prices, levels of output, GNP and the rate of growth of capacity. In the particular case of energy, these inter-action effects do not happen to be very significant.

This has important implications for energy modeling. Most energy modeling is partial equilibrium analysis that does not consider feedback from the rest of the economy. A typical model will make projections of supply and demand for some energy product based on exo-genous estimates of GNP. Our analysis shows that the feed-back effects of the individual energy sector price on the aggregate economy is probably not very large so that the assumption of exogenous GNP is reasonable.

In conclusion, it is important to distinguish be-tween the importance of the manner in which the results of this model were derived and the importance of the results themselves. The significance of the finding that the real price of energy has a relatively small effect on economic growth has been extensively discussed. The major contribution of this work, however, is that this result was derived using a general equilibrium methodology that considered all the major interactions between conditions of energy supply and economic activity. Finally, this thesis has presented a methodology that is a good general foundation for the applied study of the interaction of microeconomic phenomena and macroeconomic variables over time. An adaptation of this model that shows its basic flexibility in measuring the impact of changes in the conditions of energy supply on economic conditions is presented as an appendix to this chapter. In this case, the impact of changing conditions of electricity supply was investigated.

APPENDIX A

APPENDIX TO CHAPTER THREE

(Solution Strategy)

Solution Strategy

The growth model was presented in Chapter three as a series of mathematical equilibrium conditions. Before we can use the growth model to simulate the impact of varying conditions of energy supply on economic growth, we must specify the functional form of these mathematical relationships, make numerical assumptions about the parameters of the functions, and develop a suitable technique for solving the model. In this appendix we specify the functional form of the relations in the growth model and describe the algorithm used in solving it. Because the results of simulations are closely tied to the numerical assumptions, these assumptions are presented jointly with the results in the fifth chapter.

The growth model is simulated one year at a time. After obtaining each single year solution, certain variables representing factor supply, resource depletion and labor productivity are updated and the following year solution is initiated. The principal challenge is finding the one year solution, which requires meeting all of the short run general equilibrium conditions of a market economy. The general strategy employed in the solution is that suggested by Arrow and Starrett in their paper,

"Cost- and Demand- Theoretical Approaches to the Theory of Price Determination." [5] There they point out that any constant-returns-to-scale, non-joint-production economy can be reduced to a set of supply and demand relationships in factor markets only. We exploit this fact in the solution.

In our model ten factors of production exist, labor and the nine sector specific flows of capital services (derived from the nine sector specific capital stocks). The prices of these ten factors of production are w (the price of labor), and r_i (the prices of capital services in the nine sectors). In vector notation,

$$r = \begin{bmatrix} w \\ r_1 \\ r_2 \\ . \\ . \\ . \\ r_9 \end{bmatrix}$$

For any vector of factor prices, r, profit maximizing behavior determines the unit factor demand for labor and for the services of the different capital stocks. (The relationship between factor prices and unit primary input requirements is homogeneous of degree zero, so only relative prices are relevant. The price of labor, w, is

the numeraire.) These unit primary input requirements make
up the 10x9 matrix, b.

$$
b = \begin{bmatrix}
b_{L1} & b_{L2} & \cdot & \cdot & \cdot & b_{L9} \\
b_{K1} & 0 & \cdot & \cdot & \cdot & 0 \\
0 & b_{K2} & 0 & \cdot & \cdot & 0 \\
& & & \cdot & & \\
0 & & \cdot & & \cdot & b_{K9}
\end{bmatrix}
$$

Here the b_{Li} and the b_{Ki} are the labor and capital service
inputs necessary to produce one unit of the output of sector
i. Computationally it is easiest to derive these requirements from the duality relationships discussed in Chapter 2.

1a) $\qquad b_{Li} = \dfrac{\partial V_i(w,r_i)}{\partial w}$

1b) $\qquad b_{Ki} = \dfrac{\partial V_i(w,r_i)}{\partial r_i}$

where the $V_i(w,r_i)$ are CES unit value added functions
(analogous to unit cost functions) with the form

2) $\qquad V_i = \gamma_i [\delta \cdot w^{-\rho} + (1-\delta) r_i^{-\rho}]^{-\frac{1}{\rho}}$.

The interindustry transaction technology embodied
in the matrix A (discussed in Chapter 3), the set of

primary input prices, r, and the corresponding matrix of unit input requirements determine the prices of the produced goods, P, through the relation

3) $P = (1-A)^{-1} b'r.$

In each year the supplies of the primary inputs are fixed, so the vector of primary input prices determines GNP through the relation

4) $GNP = r'K_s.$

Here K_s is the vector of quantities of primary inputs available to the economy in any year.

GNP and prices determine the final demands for final goods and services, Y, through the relationships discussed in Chapter 3.

5) $Y = C(GNP,P) + I(GNP,P) + G(GNP,P) + X(\overline{X},P) - M(\overline{X},P)$

Final demand and the interindustry transactions matrix A determine gross output requirements, Q.

6) $Q = (I-A)^{-1}Y$

Gross output and the unit input requirements matrix b determine the primary input demands, K_d.

7) $K_d = bQ$

Equilibrium is achieved when the primary input demand vector K_d is equal to the primary input supply vector K_s. This occurs only if the equilibrium primary price vector, r, has been chosen as a starting point. Primary input demands are continuous functions of primary input prices, and when the set of primary input prices that clears the factor markets is found the model is solved for the given year.

Solving the model involves using an iterative procedure. A set of factor prices is chosen and the resulting primary input demand vector, K_d, is computed. It is then compared with the vector of factor supplies, K_s. If the excess demand for a factor is positive, its price is raised, and if the excess demand for a factor is negative, its price is lowered. Only the nine capital markets (with their associated nine prices of capital services) are examined and adjusted. The price of labor is the numeraire. Walras' law assures us that when the nine markets for capital services are in equilibrium the tenth factor market, that for labor, will also be in equilibrium.

The adjustment of the factor prices in response to excess demand is analogous to the workings of a market. Firms in each industry bid with each other to set the price or quasi rent of the services of the capital stock that

they own. However, their decisions are affected by the
prices established in the other capital service markets,
so that all prices must be adjusted simultaneously.

The price adjustment mechanism used in solving this
model depends on the ratio of demand to supply for each
factor.

$$8) \qquad r_i^N = r_i^0 \left(\frac{K_{id}}{K_{is}}\right)^h$$

Here r_i^N and r_i^0 are the new and old prices of capital
services of sector i; K_{id} and K_{is} are the demands for and
supplies of capital services in sector i, and h determines
the rate of change in prices. The larger h is, the greater
will be the response in price to a proportionate excess
demand. For any given h the price response will diminish
as demand for a factor approaches its supply.

Setting h is a practical problem in obtaining a
solution. If h is too small the system can converge so
slowly that it might not reach a solution in a reasonable
number of iterations. However, if h is too large the
resulting price changes can cause destabilizing oscillations.
Another problem is that the same h might be too high at
one point in the convergence process causing oscillation,
while it may be too low to achieve a reasonable rate of
convergence once the solution is approached. To cure the
problem the solution algorithm does 30 iterations, and

then checks to see if the system is oscillating. If so, it decreases h, to dampen the oscillations. If not, it raises h to speed up convergence. The algorithm then performs another 30 iterations and checks again for oscillation. When the amount demanded of the service of each of the nine capital goods is within 0.1% of the amount supplied, the factor markets are considered cleared.

Once the solution vector of factor prices is found in any year, the equilibrium GNP, product prices, levels of output and allocations of labor to each sector are determined. These relations make up the solution of the model for the year.

The capital stocks of the different sectors are then depreciated and the amount of investment goods produced that year are allocated to the different sectors according to the criteria developed in Chapter 4. The stock of labor available to the economy as well as its Harrod neutral technical effectiveness is increased by the exogenously given amounts g and v. Finally, the effect of the year's production of oil on depletion of reserves determines the Hicks neutral decline in productivity of primary inputs for sector 6. Once these changes take place, the model is ready to be solved for the following year. Figure 1 gives a schematic diagram of how the model reaches equilibrium for each year. The

algorithm starts with an arbitrary r, and then adjusts
r until the r for which $K_d = K_s$ is found.

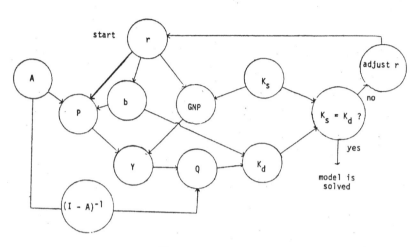

Figure 1
Solution Technique

where

r - primary input price

P - product prices

b - primary input requirements matrix

A - matrix of interindustry transactions

Y - final demand

Q - gross output

K_d - factor demand

K_s - factor supply

APPENDIX B

APPENDIX TO CHAPTER FIVE

(Other Results)

Other Results

The results that have been presented in this dissertation relate to the national economy. The model was
also used in a study of the potential effects of a nuclear
moratorium in California. This study, which was done by
the Center for Energy Studies of the University of Texas
for the Federal Energy Administration, is called "Direct
and Indirect Economic, Social and Environmental Impacts
of the Passage of the California Nuclear Power Plants
Initiative." A modified form of the national growth model
was used to evaluate the effect on economic growth in
California of more expensive electricity which might result
from restrictions on the cheapest source of electricity,
nuclear power. A description of how the national model
was adapted to the conditions of the California economy
will be given now. This description is similar to one
given in "Adaptation of the National Model to California,"
Appendix 3B, of the main report.

The basic task involved in adapting the national
model for use in an application specific to California is
the construction of a table that is comparable to Table 3
of this thesis. Estimates of the dollar value of
California's gross state product (GSP) are available from
the California Statistical Abstract, 1974 [4]. The
national figures for division of output into C, I, and G

were then used to make the appropriate decomposition for
California. These total values of final demand were then
allocated among the 9 sectors. In the case of I and G,
where final consumption of energy goods is very low,
national figures for the division were used. The
decomposition for C was made somewhat differently because
the energy intensity of consumption in California is less
than that in the country as a whole. Based on information
on both national use of energy by consumers by fuel type,
and on California use of energy by consumers by fuel type,
all available in Crump and Readling [9], the coefficients
of energy in the consumption bundle were changed as shown
in Table A1.

The adjustments were made in the following way.
Let the ratio of California's final demand by consumers
for fuel type i to the nation's total demand be r_i. Let
the ratio of California's consumption expenditures to the
national level be c. The national proportion of energy
of type i in consumption was multiplied by (r_i/c) to
derive the estimate for California of the proportion of
consumption of energy type i. The remaining consumption
proportions (sectors 1-4) were then increased so that all
proportions continued to add to one.

The coefficients of several columns of the A matrix
were changed from national figures in an exactly analogous

TABLE A1

Proportion of Energy in Final Consumption
(in 1971 dollars)

Sector	National	California
5	.000	.000
6	.000	.000
7	.023	.018
8	.016	.016
9	.009	.010

way. The changes made are shown in Table A2. The changes
for industrial use (sector 2) were made in this way. If
the ratio of California's industrial use of fuel type i to
that of the nation is r_i, and the ratio of California's
gross industrial output to that of the nation is c, the
input-output coefficient relating input of fuel type i to
industrial output was multiplied by (r_i/c). The same
procedure was used for commercial (sector 4) use.

Estimates of control totals (the Q vector) for
1967 were available from the data base of the Input-Output
Model.* These were extrapolated to 1971 using the GSP
growth rate from 1967 to 1971 for sectors 1-4. For sectors 5-9 the following procedure was used. From Crump and
Readling [9] figures on gross physical production in California of energy source i (say C_i) and national gross
physical production of that type (say N_i) were available.
If the national value of gross output from sector i is X_i,
the control total for sector i for California was
estimated as $(C_i/N_i) \cdot X_i$.

The above summarizes the changes made to the underlying data base of the national model to make it more
accurately reflect the economy of California.

---

*This is a location-quotient-adapted I-O model used in the
main report.

TABLE A2

Input-Output Coefficients

Sector 2 - Industry

Sector	National	California
5	.0036	.0000
6	.0000	.0000
7	.0069	.0030
8	.0075	.0050
9	.0055	.0040

Sector 4 - Services

Sector	National	California
5	.0001	.0000
6	.0001	.0000
7	.0058	.0010
8	.0107	.0110
9	.0021	.0040

Our analysis was done for the following three sets
of assumptions about the annual rate of growth of underlying economic factors.

	Low	Medium	High
Labor Force Growth	1.25%	2.25%	3.50%
Rate of Harrod Neutral Technical Progress	2.50%	3.00%	3.50%
Growth Rate in BAU Case (with nuclear power)	3.50%	4.90%	6.50%

These assumptions were simply meant to bracket the possible
futures. The last row is not the sum of the first two since
California was assumed not to be on a balanced growth path
due to the recent increase of OPEC prices and rapidly
escalating domestic energy costs.

In simulating the model to determine the changes
that result from going from one electricity supply scenario
to another, the results of the Regionalized Electricity
Model (REM)* were substituted as exogenous inputs for the
energy growth model's representation of electric power
(sector 8). The growth model was then simulated with these
exogenous inputs to determine the impact of changes in
electricity supply on the growth rate and other features of
the rest of the economy.

---

*This model, which was developed by Martin L. Baughman,
is a detailed model of the electrical utility sector for
California.

The substitution of the REM results was made in the following way. From the REM we took the real price and total production of electricity in each year, as well as the demand for intermediate (fuel and labor) inputs. Fuel inputs were distinguished between in-state and out-of-state sources. The real price of electricity impacted the model by working its way through the input-output mechanism and being reflected in the real prices of other goods and services. Use of imported fuel (or imported electricity itself) was modeled as a trade activity for which payment was made to out-of-state sources in output of sector 2, as in the national model. When these more expensive sources were used, consumption in California of course fell because resources were devoted to the production that paid for the imports. Finally, real capital spending of the utility sector was taken from the REM, and subtracted from the pool of investable funds available in California, as determined by the savings rate and GSP. The remainder of the funds were then allocated to the other sectors according to a slightly different investment scheme than for the national model. Gross investment was allocated in direct proportion to total profits.

The REM gave detailed projections of supply and demand for electricity through 1995 for three scenarios;

the scenarios were no constraints on nuclear power, out
of state coal substituting for nuclear power, and imported
oil substituting for nuclear power. These scenarios
correspond to business as usual, increased reliance on
coal and increased reliance on oil. In the worst case
in terms of the cost of electricity generation, reliance
on imported oil, the real price of electricity was 25%
higher in 1995 than in the business as usual case. The
effect of this higher cost of electricity on economic
growth is minimal, and the growth rate of consumption is
reduced by only .03 percent below the business as usual
case.

The appendix demonstrates the flexibility of the
basic growth model in simulating the effect of changes
in different types of energy supply. It also shows how
the results of more detailed models of individual sectors
can be meshed into this model's general equilibrium
framework.

REFERENCES

[1]   Almon, Clopper, Jr., et al. 1985 Interindustry Fore-
      casts of the American Economy. Lexington:
      Lexington Books, 1974.

[2]   Almon, S. "The Distributed Lag Between Capital Appro-
      priations and Expenditures." Econometrica, Vol. 33,
      No. 1 (January 1965), pp. 178-96.

[3]   Anderson, W.H.L. "Business Fixed Investment: A
      Marriage of Fact and Fancy" in Ferber, R., ed.
      Determinants of Investment Behavior. Universities
      National Bureau Conference Series, No. 18. New
      York: Columbia University Press for National
      Bureau of Economic Research, 1967.

[4]   _____. Corporate Finance, and Fixed Invest-
      ment, an Econometric Study. Boston: Division of
      Research, Graduate School of Business Administra-
      tion, Harvard University, 1964.

[5]   Arrow, K. J., and Starrett, D.A. "Cost and Demand
      Theoretical Approaches to the Theory of Price
      Determination." (Discussion Paper No. 201)
      Harvard Institute of Economic Research, 1971.

[6]   Bourneuf, A. "Manufacturing Investment, Excess Capa-
      city and the Rate of Growth of Output." American
      Economic Review, Vol. 54, No. 4 (September 1964),
      pp. 607-25.

[7]   Christ, Carl F., Mansfield, Edwin, and Borch, Karl.
      "Discussion - Topics in Economic Theory," American
      Economic Review, Vol. 53, No. 2 (May 1962),
      pp. 269-74.

[8]   Christensen, L. R., Jorgenson, D.W., and Lau, L. J.
      "Transcendental Logarithmic Production Frontiers."
      Review of Economics and Statistics, Vol. 55
      (February 1973), pp. 28-55.

[9]   Crump, L. H. and Readling, C. L. Fuel and Energy Data:
      United States by States and Regions, 1973.
      Washington, D.C.: U.S. Bureau of Mines, U.S.
      Government Printing Office, 1974.

[10] Data Resources, Inc. DRI Computer User's Manual
      for the Generalized Interindustry Transactions
      Model. Cambridge, 1972.

[11] Diewert, W. E. "An Application of the Shepard
      Duality Theorem: A Generalized Leontief Production
      Function." Journal of Political Economy, Vol. 79
      (May/June 1971), pp. 481-507.

[12] Eisner, R. "Capital Expenditures, Profits and the
      Acceleration Principle" in Models of Income
      Determination. Studies in Income and Wealth,
      Vol. 28. Princeton: Princeton University Press,
      1964.

[13] _____. "A Distributed Lag Investment Function."
      Econometrica, Vol. 28, No. 1 (January 1960), pp. 1-
      29.

[14] _____. "Investment Fact and Fancy." American
      Economic Review, Vol. 53, No. 2 (May 1963),
      pp. 237-46.

[15] _____. "Investment Pland and Realizations."
      American Economic Review, Vol. 52, No. 2 (May 1962),
      pp. 190-203.

[16] _____. "A Permanent Income Theory for Investment."
      American Economic Review, Vol. 57, No. 3 (June
      1967), pp. 363-90.

[17] _____. "Realization of Investment Anticipations"
      in Duesenberry, J., Fromm, G., Klein, L. R. and
      Kuh, E., eds., The Brookings Quarterly Model of
      the United States. Amsterdam: North Holland, 1965.

[18] Evans, M. K. "A Study of Industry Investment Deci-
      sions." Review of Economics and Statistics,
      Vol. 49, No. 2 (May 1967), pp. 151-64.

[19] Fried, E. R. and Schulze, C. L., eds. Higher Oil
      Prices and the World Economy. Washington, D.C.:
      The Brookings Institution, 1975.

[20] Federal Energy Administration. Project Independence
      Report, 1974. Washington, D.C.: U.S. Government
      Printing Office, 1974.

[21] Gould, J. P. "The Use of Endogenous Variables in
      Dynamic Models of Investment." Quarterly Journal
      of Economics, Vol. 83, No. 4 (November 1969)
      pp. 580-99.

[22] Gunning, J. W., Osterrieth, M., and Waelbroeck, J.
      "The Price of Energy and Potential Growth of
      Developed Countries, an Attempt at Qualification."
      World Bank, 1975. (Miemographed)

[23] Heilbroner, R. "Middle-Class Myths, Middle-Class
      Realities." Atlantic Monthly, August, 1976, p. 41.

[24] Hickman, B. Investment Demand the U.S. Economic
      Growth. Washington, D.C.: The Brookings Insti-
      tution, 1965.

[25] Hnyilicza, E. "An Aggregate Model of Energy and Eco-
      nomic Growth." M.I.T. Energy Laboratory Working
      Paper No. MIT-EL75-010WP, August, 1975.

[26] Hotelling, H. "The Economics of Exhaustible Resources."
      Journal of Political Economy, Vol. 39 (April 1931),
      pp. 137-75.

[27] Hudson, E. A. and Jorgenson, D. W. "Interindustry
      Transactions" in Jorgenson, D.W., Berndt, E. R.,
      and Hudson, E. A., U.S. Energy Resources and
      Economic Growth. Final Report to the Energy Policy
      Project. Washington, D.C., 1973.

[28] _____. "U.S. Energy Policy and Economic
      Growth, 1975-2000." The Bell Journal of Economics
      and Management Science, Vol. 5, No. 2 (Autumn
      1974), pp. 461-514.

[29] Jorgenson, D.W. "Anticipations and Investment
      Behavior" in Duesenberry, J. S., Fromm, G., Klein,
      L. R. and Kuh, E., eds. The Brookings Quarterly
      Model of the United States. Amsterdam:
      North Holland, 1965.

[30] _____. "Capital Theory and Investment Behavior."
      American Economic Review, Vol. 53, No. 2 (May 1963),
      pp. 247-59.

[31] _____. "Econometric Studies of Investment
      Behavior: A Survey." Journal of Economic Litera-
      ture, Vol. 9, No. 4 (December 1971), pp. 1111-47.

[32] _____. "Rational Distributed Lag Functions."
Econometrica, Vol. 32, No. 1 (January 1966),
pp. 135-49.

[33] Jorgenson, D. W., Hunter, J. and Nadiri, M. I. "A
Comparison of Alternative Econometric Models of
Corporate Investment Behavior." Econometrica,
Vol. 38, No. 2 (March 1970), pp. 187-212.

[34] _____. "The Predictive Performance of Econometric Models of Quarterly Investment Behavior."
Econometrica, Vol. 38, No. 2 (March 1970),
pp. 213-24.

[35] Jorgenson, D. W. and Stephenson, J. A. "Investment
Behavior in U.S. Manufacturing, 1947-1960."
Econometrica, Vol. 35, No. 2 (April 1967), pp. 169-
220.

[36] Meyer, J. and Glauber, R. Investment Decisions,
Economic Forecasting and Public Policy. Boston:
Division of Research, Graduate School of Business
Administration, Harvard University, 1964.

[37] Organization for Economic Co-operation and Development. Energy Prospects to 1985. Paris: OECD,
1975.

[38] Resek, R. W. "Investment by Manufacturing Firms: A
Quarterly Time Series Analysis of Industry Data."
Review of Economics and Statistics, Vol. 48, No. 3
(August 1966), pp. 322-33.

[39] Shepard, R. W. Cost and Production Functions.
Princeton: Princeton University Press, 1953.

[40] Solow, R. M. Growth Theory, and Exposition. New York:
Oxford University Press, 1970.

[41] State of California. California Statistical Abstract,
1974. Sacramento, 1975.

For Product Safety Concerns and Information please contact our EU
representative GPSR@taylorandfrancis.com Taylor & Francis Verlag GmbH,
Kaufingerstraße 24, 80331 München, Germany

Printed and bound by CPI Group (UK) Ltd, Croydon, CR0 4YY
08/05/2025
01864397-0003